CONCILIUM

CONCILIUM

RETHINKING EUROPE

Edited by
Alberto Melloni and Janet Martin Soskice

SCM Press · London

Published by SCM Press, 9–17 St Albans Place, London N1 0NX

Copyright © Stichting Concilium

English translations copyright © 2004 SCM-Canterbury Press Ltd

All rights reserved. No part of this publication may be
reproduced, stored in a retrieval system, or transmitted,
in any form or by any means, electronic, mechanical, photocopying,
recording or otherwise, without the prior written permission of
Stichting Concilium, Erasmusplein 1,
6525 HT Nijmegen, The Netherlands

ISBN 0 334 03078 1

Printed by Biddles Ltd, Guildford and King's Lynn

Concilium Published February, April, June, October
December

Contents

Introduction
    JANET MARTIN SOSKICE WITH ALBERTO MELLONI   7

I. The Language For Europe: Myth And Reality

Understanding Europe
    ROMAN SIEBENROCK   11

Images of Europe and Challenges of Europe for the Church:
Catholicism in Recent History
    ALBERTO MELLONI   22

The 'New' Europe: A Spiritual Gesture
    ERIK BORGMAN   33

From Tolerance to Rights: Religions in the Unification Process
    SILVIO FERRARI   42

II. Europe, Christianity and Religions

Judaism and Europe: History and Counter-History
    MICHAEL BRENNER   51

The Ecumenical Movement in Europe: Challenges and Conflicts
    REINHARD FRIELING   57

Euro-Islam: Challenge or Opportunity?
    KARL-JOSEF KUSCHEL   67

III. Theological Challenge

Does Europe Jeopardize the De-Europeanization (and Purification) of the Church?
JAMES K. VOISS, SJ   77

A European Civil Religion?
GIUSEPPE RUGGIERI   86

Christianity in a Multi-Religious Europe
THOMAS BREMER   95

IV. Excursuses

Post-Communist Europe and the Continued Existence of Atheism
MIKLÓS TOMKA   105

Russia: Europe or Not?
VLADIMIR FEDOROV   114

John Paul II, Poland and Europe
PATRICK MICHEL   124

Documentation
Online Documentation on the Churches and Religions in the European Union
MASSIMO FAGGIOLI   129

Contributors   135

Introduction

JANET MARTIN SOSKICE WITH ALBERTO MELLONI

In Europe, home to some of the world's oldest nation states, a new political reality is emerging. The trauma of two world wars and the ugly flowering of genocide in nations whose proud boast was to have spread Christianity through the world caused searching reappraisal in their aftermath. According to Hippolyte Simon, present Bishop of Clermont-Ferraud, the Coal and Steel agreement of 1951 was, amongst its more tangible aspects, also a 'spiritual gesture' whose significance was 'never again' – never again to war, to genocide, to fraternal slaughter. Christian politicians and trade unionists were amongst the prominent architects of the new Union after the war, motivated to activism by their Christian faith.

Yet the Coal and Steel agreement was a relatively easy initial step. Awareness of the depth of diversity in their respective national pasts mean that 'never again' has to be said frequently, and some of these 'never agains' involve religions and churches.

Europeans are now a little indolent when it comes to putting together their faith with their politics. Confusion reigns – should the European Christian citizen be happy with the new polity? Unflagging in support for what is still a fragile agreement? Within the Catholic Church, the Pope has given sustained support to this new venture, although not without hopes of his own as to its outcome. All agree that Europeans stand at an important historic juncture. Opinions vary as to what the end of this shared adventure should be; should one wish for a United States of Europe, or a loose conglomeration with shared economic, social and geo-political policies? The fact of the matter is that, whatever individual preferences, the European Union is a reality affecting the lives of all those who live within its bounds, and with the potential to affect many who do not. Gone are the franc, the mark and the drachma – the euro has replaced some of the oldest 'common coin' in circulation. A European Parliament runs alongside national parliaments. Labour moves freely across all those Western lands once conquered by Rome. With the 2004 accession of new member states, including Hungary and Poland, we have the end of fifty years of a cruel East-West divide. Europe itself is 'a new West'.

Europe will have unified policies on immigration, refugees, trade relations and Third World debt. The changes underway affect not only the economics and politics but the self-understanding of European citizenry. Is this new Europe going to be any more 'Christian' than the old one? What should the world want from Europe and how should Europeans understand themselves in this new political incarnation (Borgman)? For readers of *Concilium* this will also imply questions of faith and history, and questions of guiding symbolism.

What is Europe, after all? Australia, Africa and the Americas are clearly demarcated by the boundary of the sea. Europe, by contrast, has no such evident marks of demarcation, at least on its eastern side. The nineteenth-century Russian philosopher, Danilevsky, asked if what we call Europe is not 'just a peninsula at the end of Asia . . . a glamourous word . . .' but perhaps, he suggests, an empty one (Fedorov). This is why the grounding metaphors or symbols of Europe are so important. Is Europe a shared house, a set of lungs, a tree with common roots and later grafted branches (Melloni, Siebenrock)? If Europe is such because of its shared 'roots', then why do these same roots nourish Turkey, but not Russia? If Europe has two lungs, will it need always be divided, spiritually if not economically, into an East and West (Melloni). How we conceive of Europe will play a major part in what Europe becomes, and here enter matters of faith and history.

Europe is widely considered to be the cradle of Christianity – widely, but wrongly. As 150 years of biblical criticism have made clear, Christianity is a profoundly Oriental, or at least Middle Eastern faith, albeit one whose origins lay in the Greek-speaking and Hellenized remains of the empire of Alexander. Christianity spread most quickly across north Africa – to Egypt, Libya, what is now Tunisia – and with equal speed throughout what is now Turkey, Afghanistan, Iraq and Iran. By 245 AD, when most northern Europeans were still running around kidnapping their brides, there were already twenty-four Christian bishoprics in the Tigris-Euphrates valley. Hungary, by contrast, was not Christianized until the year 1000.

We think Europe to be the centre of Christianity only because our historic memories are short. Saint Zeno, the African missionary who converted the population of Verona to Christianity, and whose very black and African Byzantine image stands as tribute in his namesake church there, would have been astonished to think of Christianity as a European faith. Indeed African and Asian Christians have more than good reason to think Europe was never more than superficially Christianized, given its subsequent political and social history.

The election in the last quarter of the twentieth century of a Polish pope, the first non-Italian pope in many centuries, has had important consequences for Europe, and for the Catholic Church. Although the ink is not dry on the history of the late twentieth century, most political historians agree that the role of Poland, reinforced by its famous native son in Rome, was decisive in the breakdown of the communist East (Tomka, Michel). But if the pope has been important to Europe, then Europe has been important to the pope. From the beginning, the pontificate of John Paul II has had as one of its concerns the uniting of a wounded and divided Europe. The dynamics of East and West have played an important role. Papal writings have used a plenitude of images (lungs, roots, house) to try to set forth a vision. Perhaps, as in the diversity of images Paul uses to explain the Atonement, we need a set of overlapping metaphors to appreciate our shared past and tentative future?

The common 'roots' of European nations is not an appealing metaphor if one considers these must somehow tangle around the Shoah. Even though full-blown Nazism was an atheistic and anti-Christian ideology, the fact remains that European nations, East and West, colluded in the destruction of their Jewish citizenry. The shadow of the Shoah still hangs over Europe (Brenner). That this should have happened in 'Christian' Europe is a blow to the heart of faith, yet a reminder to Christians everywhere how readily ethnic and religious bitterness can slide into hostilities, or just fatal indifference.

Today Christianity is for most Europeans part of Europe's distant past and not much more. The new political and economic union, as part of its turn away from a divided past, has decided to refrain from any reference to Christianity in its constitution. This could be conceived as a generous gesture towards the numbers of European citizens who are of other faiths, its Muslims and its Jews, but it is probably more a deliberate distancing of the secular society from its religious past. The inter-Christian rivalry which broke out into bloody violence with the Wars of Religion have not been forgotten by secular authorities (Frieling, Ferrari). Religion, the new Europe seems to say, is of our past, not for our present or future. Of course few Europeans, least of all members of the major Christian denominations, would like a return to the mediaeval 'Christendom' with its conflation of Christian identity and European politics. Indeed the churches have been amongst the first to argue that Europe's Christian past should not be used as a metaphorical lever against its immigrant minorities (Kuschel). On the other hand, belief in God, and belief in the God of Abraham, Isaac and Jacob, is dear to many of Europe's new immigrants, as well as its old citizenry, and many of these non-Christians are equally alarmed at the extent to which the legislating bodies seem eager to paint God out of Europe's collective social and religious past.

It cannot be doubted that Christianity has contributed hugely to the mix of values, ideals, and hopes taken for granted by European citizenry today. The history of Europe does not make sense without the history of Christianity, in all its strengths and weaknesses: the importance of the individual, ideals of freedom and self-determination, commitment to the common good and to the dignity of women, the very old, the very young – all these have a deep anchorage in Europe's Christian past. It is not unreasonable for religious people, and not just Christians, to wonder if they will have a place in its secularized and commericalized future (Ruggieri).

What then should the world want from Europe (Riccardi, Voiss)? The purpose of this volume is bring a double lens – historical and theological – to bear on Europe. We hope the essays contained here will unfold some of the challenges to church and faith, some of the semantic vagaries of over-used terms and images (roots and lungs, values and rights) and remind us of key Christian concepts that seem often forgotten in the political process (forgiveness, consolation, healing, poverty). Despite some palpable achievements it is too early for celebration and cheap, optimistic prophecies. To offer good questions is a beginning.

I. The Language for Europe: Myth and Reality

Understanding Europe

ROMAN SIEBENROCK

Europe is the historical force which has made, and is still making, the most substantial contribution to shaping and changing today's world. Purely in geographical terms, Europe is not a land mass that can be clearly defined. From this perspective it is only an appendix to Asia. Purely in geographical terms, Europe is a continent only because Europe is more than a geographical designation. 'Europe' is not identical with the 'West'; on the contrary Europe has two lungs; if it is not used as an ideological slogan, the term 'the West with one lung' refers to Western, Latin Christianity and the Germanic peoples. The exceptions of Poland and Hungary confirm this. Therefore even the European Union in 2004 will in fact embrace only the West; as an exception, Greece remains a dangerous memory of the greater unity. But Europe means more.

I can approach 'Europe' only from different perspectives which I shall attempt to present as questions. It is inevitable that what I venture to describe as touches of Europe can also be found elsewhere. Of course we find science and universities, urban cultures, middle class and aristocracy, conflicts and monotheistic religions, in many other places. However, it is not the individual touch that seems to me to make up Europe, but the diverse mixture of various aspects and the radical nature of the development of them into a permanent ambivalence which time and again keeps coming to a head. Europe represents the extreme of an experiment in human history.

I. Where is Europe?

This simple question contains the whole puzzle. 'Europe' seems to denote the Western part of Asia bounded by the Urals and the Caspian Sea in the

East; the Arctic Ocean in the north; the Caucasus, the Black Sea and the Mediterranean in the south; and the Atlantic in the West. But some islands of the continental peninsula reach as far as America and Africa. And for a long time there have been Europeans almost all over the world in considerable numbers and diversity: Italians, Irish, Iberians, English – one would have to mention almost every country. If one goes on to single out those powers and forces which have emanated from Europe like art, music, architecture and also philosophies, sciences, legal notions and capitalism, the question can only be: 'Where isn't Europe?' In territorial terms the question becomes a banal one and so gets no answer. But intellectually the horizon is boundless. We must ask a different question if we are not to assume that Europe is simply everything.

II. How has Europe become what it is today?

If 'Europe' is never merely a geographical designation but can be understood only as an intellectual construction, a complex idea with countless aspects and relationships, then in origin and development it can always be understood only as a historical structure. So the complex of questions through which we are to consider Europe must be divided into three parts, which I shall discuss one by one.

1. Where does Europe come from?

What are the origins of Europe and what historical guidelines do these origins give? Not everything that has taken place on European territory is to be called 'Europe' or 'European'. Moreover the chronological beginning can be put at different times. I think that it is meaningful to associate Europe and modernity, and therefore put the fifteenth century as the European watershed. The decisive argument for this is the final fall of Rome (East Rome) with the conquest of Constantinople in 1453 and the beginning of an autonomous and independent development in this part of the world. Because I do not identify Europe with the 'West', the Western concept of the Middle Ages is inadequate for defining Europe. East and West have always been part of Europe.

Europe seems primarily to have four roots: the Germanic and Slav peoples, Christianity and the monotheistic tradition, Greece and Rome. Europe grew from this four-fold heritage. The migration of Germanic and Slavonic peoples threw the original populations of the regions into turmoil and sparked off a migratory movement which never stopped. These people took on a special character by accepting the cultures of the Mediterranean countries which they conquered. Europe came into being in a comprehensive process of cultural adoption. Christianity proved to be the determining factor in this process; it was accepted in its Arian variants by the Goths and in its Catholic version by the Franks, originally without compulsion. The first mission to the Slavs by Cyril and Methodius and above all the adoption of Byzantine Christianity by Rus in Kiev was a voluntary decision. However, the Christianity adopted was itself a cultural symbiosis.

Those who accepted Christianity also took on the memory of Israel, and the split between Christians and Jews which already lay back in antiquity. The image of itself which Europe formed was shaped by the person of Jesus of Nazareth; the Bible moulded languages and thought; and the notion of the supreme and the transcendent, with all its heretical deviations, developed from the God of Jesus Christ. However, the two great ancient cultures of Greece and Rome were equally effective in handing down belief, indeed even more so: Christianity was communicated in either its Roman Latin or its Greek form.

Greece means philosophy and science as the question of the truth and the form of the good, rational life. The Socratic art of questioning, the Platonic longing for the eternally divine in the divinization of human beings, Aristotelian science with its orientation on the world of the senses, but also scepticism, a Cynic contempt for the world and Stoic universality, and the beginnings of an ethic of humankind, were present. Greek thought is an indispensable enlightenment in the quest for the light as the truth of being and living. The love of truth ('philosophy') will be stronger than life lived by habit and tradition which is not reflected on and above all stronger than authority to which no thought is given.

Rome's talent was for political organization, which is its main legacy alongside language, the alphabet, the will to power, and law. Not only did the German emperors see themselves as successors to the Roman empire; Moscow claimed to be the third Rome. Thus the antagonism between East and West, which goes back as far as the division of the Roman empire in the third century, became a determining hallmark of Europe.

The two other Abrahamic monotheisms gained influence in Europe only in connection with Christianity. Judaism remained more tolerated than desired; it was persecuted time and again, especially in the watershed period mentioned above, and not just in Spain. Jews continued to be stigmatized as potential scapegoats. Antisemitism is not an incidental phenomenon; its distinctive characteristic is that it flourishes even without Jews. Islam represents not only a threat but also a teacher in its communication of Greek philosophy, mathematics, administration and trade.

Roots are the foundation but not yet the form. Europe comes into view only in the way in which these beginnings take effect. But what are the determining forces of development? What factors can be distinguished? No one around, say, 1000 could have foreseen that this 'starving Europe', characterized above all by primal forest, would become the key continent of the second millennium. Yet the key development began just after the end of the first millennium. The decisive factor of this whole development is the differentiation of society, motivated by a solemn sense of freedom; this begins with the antagonism between pope and emperor and soon shows itself in the struggle for autonomy, in cities, universities and various religious orders. The autonomous and federal pluralization of society, and above all the distinction between spiritual and secular power in its antagonism and tense relationships, shaped the distinctive characteristics of (Western) European history. Only under the conditions of recognized political and cultural autonomies, which were also called for radically, could the other forces develop.

A second force that needs to be mentioned is science and thought, particularly in its permanent readiness to cross boundaries as a matter or principle. Thinking means questions and radical criticism. The special mark of European thought is a radical criticism which is directed not only against all external claims but also against itself; in the process it rejects any flight from or surrender to tradition, faith or authority. The restless heart that Augustine left behind at the beginning of his *Confessions* as a legacy to the European self-understanding meant that even God himself would soon no longer be able to give people peace. Science arises out of radical questions about what is real and true. Therefore thought also puts every possible question to faith. Without needing to, Anselm of Canterbury developed his examination of faith by means of the criterion of autonomous reason: without Christ (*remoto Christo*) and with an appeal to necessary reasons (*rationes necessariae*). The eighteenth-century Enlightenment was not the first to have a dispute over the faculties and exercise 'autonomous' thought; these can already be found in scholasticism.

A third force which settled first in the cities and city states by the sea was trade and the rise of capitalism .The great discoveries were ventured and intensified for trading purposes as well as with scientific ambition. They made use of science, and indeed furthered it: since Francis Bacon, economics, society and science have been a project for the whole of society. The inexorable advance of the explorers not only extended the geographical picture of the world but also overthrew it, as it inevitably broke up the intellectual world-view (albeit with a time-lag). This was an unprecedented event. With the extension of history and experience the current criteria became weaker. The expansion of knowledge seemed to be a value in itself. Orientation was in short supply, and human beings became nomads of the spirit. Montaigne's essays spell out this contour in exemplary fashion to the present day.

The discovery of the subject as individual awareness, as distinct from nature and society, in its freedom and exposure, its dependence and normativeness, in other words in all its ambivalence, needs to be stressed particularly as a further factor. The awakening of individual consciousness made possible a variety of guidelines: the infinite value of the individual as a result of belief in the incarnation of God (an abiding principle through all anthropological shifts), the mystical traditions of an individual piety directed to Jesus as a child in the manger, as the sufferer and in his relationship to the individual's soul as bride; the compulsory examination of the conscience in the confessional since 1215; the notion of the human being as a second creator; the rediscovery of the art and humanism of antiquity; and also the dethronement by modernity of the Middle Ages, which seemed to be nothing but gloom. The human being, the present-day human being, became the measure of all things. God may have become a human being, but now human beings confidently take the place of God.

One last, more hidden, force must not be overlooked. It is one that has driven Europe from the beginning, namely the power exercised by traumatic anxieties born of the experience of unspeakable catastrophes. It was perhaps first expressed in the myth of Europa, abducted and deceived, who met a watery grave. By this I mean not only that before industrialization Europe was always a continent marked by hunger, but that for example the plague which ravaged Europe at regular intervals from the fourteenth century on has become a metaphor for more than an internal threat. The recollection of foreign conquests continues to be a force in East and West, in different perspectives. Whereas in the East and West there has been a memory of the hordes of horsemen from the East or of the Arab armies, the conquest of Byzantium by the Crusaders in 1204 remains a trauma of Orthodoxy (which is also cultivated). On the other hand the late Middle Ages was anything but a stable time. For the church it was marked in the West by schisms which prevented the council that strove for unity with the East from really succeeding. Indeed, even to the benevolent Nicholas of Cusa the church seemed internally resistant to all reform. Europe came into being with an awareness of the radical fragility of all human relationships. It was born out of crisis.

To have a correct understanding of developments in Europe it is essential to realize that these various factors are not capable of simply being directed politically, but that time and again they become a 'critical mass'; they have to develop dynamically and rearrange themselves. Europe is just as much governed by spiritual values, guidelines and convictions as it is by conflicts and wars, with perpetual boundary violations and ventures. It has also developed from its hidden anxieties and an individualistic exaltation of itself which can take the form not only of arrogance but also of radical (self-) criticism. Expansion and unrest are the only abiding factors.

2. *How has Europe developed?*

A historical idea can be understood only from its history. One can dismiss such an attempt from the start as aberrant. Nevertheless it must be made. There can be no question of giving a summary of European history here; that would be arrogant. But I can point to the development of those factors which I defined earlier as basic forces. I suggest that European history should be read as an experiment in these different factors. Here two aspects play the main role. First there is the balance of power, which has never really been achieved successfully; secondly, time and again there is the quest for an idea of unity and cohesion, since with the Reformation and then the European wars of religion the common Christian bond was finally torn apart or proved itself incapable of producing cohesion and peace. The tragedy of Christianity in Europe lies in its inability to achieve peace at the beginning of modern times. As confessional Christianity it could only form opposing parties, and could not establish any unity which transcended states, groups and interests. This quest for a commonality also remains bound up in a cryptic, heretical way with the loss of faith, because the various surrogates have always had religious connotations. To this degree Europe is always productive of religion and elevates the maxims of its action to the level of the divine: the subject, anthropology in the mode of human rights with a claim to absolute validity, nation, class, progress, and today the market.

Socially the process of differentiation became a revolutionary force in connection with the growing awareness of individual freedom. If it began in the Investiture Dispute with the call for the freedom of the church, under the banner of the freedom of the Christian it rose up powerfully in the Reformation against tradition and against all church and state authorities. The various Reformation emigrations, above all to America, had more effect on world history than the establishment of Protestantism on the continent of Europe under various local rulers. The demand for freedom made by citizens in the American and French Revolutions continued this development. Freedom became popular, democratic. The Russian Revolution cannot be understood along these lines, because it did not establish freedom, but the collective. Only the 1989 revolution can be classed with this development, even if for a long time collectivism steadily destroyed the moral presupposition for a free democracy. But the process of differentiation embraced all other social spheres because a priori both the individual and science and the market had autonomous roots. After the idea of unity in the nation, the key force behind which was always the military, had been established in a powerful and militant way by the French Revolution as the unitive bond of society, this idea initially contradicted itself by the collective suicide attempts of Europe in two world wars. However, other surrogates like the proletariat, race or particular social groups could take the place of the lost religion: political religions as substitute religion.

The idea of European union grew out of terror in the face of these excesses. On the other hand the revolutionary processes of differentiation have become individualized: today the individual is catching up with the example of the absolutist ruler in the eighteenth century – individuals are themselves the state, morality, each by God's grace. A last (pseudo-) sovereignty is now suggested to us by the apparent rule of the consumer ('the customer as king'), which is being established on all levels. What is only apparently unlimited choice suggests boundless freedom, and here the old demand for obedience has long been replaced with disturbing success by the sublime sciences of manipulation and forecasting in marketing strategies. Such kings do not obey, but they are predictable.

Granted, science and thought were never independent solely in respect of their material presuppositions, but in relation to politics and morality they were extremely concerned for their autonomy. For a long time they fed on the roots of faith, and in dissociating themselves from those roots are perhaps even doing so today. They cannot be understood as mere instruments and tools; they are part of a comprehensive experiment of human beings with themselves. Modern science is always a matter of application, shaping and subjecting the world. But the process of knowledge is accompanied by a permanent and radical critique. This process is characterized not by the possession of truth but by the progressive refutation of views and their application to human beings. Thus human beings as little gods fall headlong from the heaven of the crown of creation into the nothingness of a complex machine.

In the twentieth century, with nuclear physics and genetic research, science has finally made it clear that it represents a permanent transgression of taboos. Moral reflections in accordance with the motto 'May we do all that we can do?' are at best placebos, because whether something can be done can be clarified only by an experiment, and science is impossible without empowering experiments. So science has given potential power into our hands which constantly surpasses itself, and which after an unforeseeable period puts human beings in question. Their very existence has already become questionable. But this process simply cannot be directed. 'Self-organization' is a term meant to bring reassurance. The case of Galileo was the last attempt to tame science politically; it was inevitable that it should fail.

However, philosophical thought, too, which is in principle radical, has lived up to its principles in the intensified crossing of boundaries. European thought is characterized not only by criticism of the Christian faith and readiness for a comprehensive critique of religion, but above all by the claim that it can venture on and propagate very diverse experiments with life, and criticize all orientations and values. If the fanfare of science was progress for all and thus the view that the light of Europe might be lit all over the world (as indeed it was), the critique of all myths is an inexorably radical critique of the European Enlightenment as imperialism grew from the same roots. Are there sharper critics of Europe than the Europeans?

Science was from the beginning bound up with trade, the market and the monetary economy. Since the industrial revolution this network has not only grown stronger but has become one-sidedly denser: science should be applied science and make a profit. Science as a guarantee of asserting oneself on the world market has become a war with other means, and the university, reformed along economic guidelines, has become the training camp. European colonialism and imperialism developed not only the earliest form of globalization ('world trade') but also progressively brought all spheres of life under its aegis, from the leisure industry to spiritual enterprises in the sphere of wellness. Free trade had appeared with the claim that it would bring prosperity for all nations, and thus renewed the unfulfilled promise.

Anxieties have changed, but they have not disappeared. Nature no longer drives us with its hidden dangers, even if Aids, Sars and earthquakes revive the old traumas: we have become uncanny to ourselves. Human beings have become riddles, threats and questions to themselves. We have already become so satiated that the vision of the superman today is ever more clearly beginning to transform itself into technical solutions for a post-biological existence. The human building site has opened, and radical manipulation knows no intrinsic bounds. Human beings can do anything. In technological dreams the old gnostic satiation with being human is itself becoming a technological prospect.

3. Common characteristics?

Can any general characteristics of these different developments be described? The main formal characteristic of the whole development is ambivalence. Enlightenment and the deepest superstition, science and esotericism, or rationality and magic, not only come together in the one society, indeed in the one person; they even seem to encourage each other. The European self-understanding is also permeated with radical ambivalence: hybris and imperialistic arrogance go along with the most radical self-criticism and unfathomable scepticism. The antagonism can also be read off relationships to others and to oneself: the annihilation and romanticizing of other cultures continue side by side, as an attempt to appropriate for oneself all forms of life in human history. Those who complain about the plundering of other cultures by the Europeans should not overlook the fact that the same Europeans have not dealt gently with themselves. Democracy, the proclamation of human rights and the philosophical foundation for the extraordinary dignity of the individual are contemporaneous with totalitarianism and fascism. There is always the danger that forms of life will turn into their opposites.

However, the spiritual bond has bidden farewell to 'post- and anti-Christian' Europe. Therefore the second characteristic is to be identified as the radical quality of the development of individual forces: the accentuation of ambivalence and antagonism. Science, individualism, the market and capital have developed to extremes. European history seems unsuited for a peaceful balance: it represents a permanent transgression of boundaries. Is this because of the theological peculiarity which marks out Europe? As I remarked, Europe does not have its roots in itself. Furthermore, Europe is not the breeding ground for a world religion. Europe is infertile where religion is concerned. Is that why so many substitute religions have to be created? Is the reason why we Europeans cannot accept this gift that, if we did, as a first intellectual response we would have to give thanks? Is perhaps our European history a great experiment in Pelagianism, which does not want to receive as a gift what is offered to it and handed on as a legacy?

III. What about Europe today?

With the Second World War, the end of colonialism and the multipolarity of the world powers, political Europe dropped out of the centre of history. It had to register a divided history of success in the second millennium. It has exported itself, its people and its ideas all over the world, and even nationalism has been taken up in a great variety of cultures, not to mention science and capitalism and other ideologies. Thus Europe seems able to congratulate itself on its 'success'. On the other hand, its history of disaster as a radical criticism from outside rebounds on it so firmly that it is apparently the greatest spectre in world history, even though it sometimes seems paralysed. The recollection of the discovery of America in the last 200 years could clarify this. Who do not orientate themselves on human rights and democracy, the constitutional state, and social and political models of a pluralistic order? On the other hand many European peoples are growing very old and beginning to die out. Our continent no longer seems capable of going on living. And how can one live without faith, hope and love?

Perhaps an indeterminate sense of a secular apocalyptic underlies this. We are in a position to bring about the end of humankind. The pattern of life exported from Europe has no future. Modern society not only lives by values which it does not itself produce, but destroys those very values on which it absolutely depends. The fundamental values of modern society, namely freedom, human dignity and rights, are being eroded from two sides. The individualism whose contours are accentuated by the cultivation of an unlimited capitalism is destroying the fundamental values of solidarity and justice. Modern science, on the other hand, cannot in principle spell out human dignity and freedom, and has transformed its formal and functional primacy of method to human beings' descriptions of themselves. How can a complex, optimizing system claim unconditional value?

However, from the greatest catastrophe in European history there arose one of the most remarkable projects in the modern history of the world: the process of European union. We have already forgotten that the idea of a European Union originally had strong Catholic roots: the notion of a transnational identity derived from the experience of a world church. But this project seems increasingly to be in crisis, the more strongly mere pragmatism reigns and the memory of the spectres in our own history pale. The draft of the European Constitution is both lacking in memory and light-footed. Who still believes in European reason after the catastrophes of the twentieth century?

We stand at the beginning of a clash with the last great ideology of the nineteenth century, technocratic capitalism. Its political colours are interchangeable. This smart totalitarianism, decked out in such an alluring way, is dangerous from two perspectives. Even among intellectual élites there is virtually no alternative to its ideas of organization. Rather, it has also conquered the spheres of education and culture at headlong speed. Secondly, together with philosophical naturalism, it has found its way into the self-descriptions of individuals, who no longer explain themselves as free beings but as complex functioning units. The total entertainment provided by the media includes these dreams and ideas in its beautiful new world.

It is clear that here any faith which contradicts and offers alternatives must be stopped in its tracks. Wellness religions are called for, and not too meagre ones. Claims by faith which require people to say yes and no and which call for radical new thought are dangerous in principle, because they always develop the potential to put current issues in question. So their truth-claims must be toned down. The Christian faith, too, has sometimes fallen victim to the equalization of all ideas of faith without putting up any opposition worth mentioning. Our own history, which is constantly held up before us, also paralyses us.

If it is to meet this challenge, European theology must go on learning. Our theology is still paralysed either by a political naivety or by the ecclesial narcissism of mock battles between theologians. For the decisive challenge for Europe will come when it really begins to grow together from East and West and the way in which we are destroying our patterns of life can no longer be concealed. Then at the latest the merely technocratic pragmatism of the logic of the stock exchange will come to an end. The statement 'If you do not believe, you will not abide' (Isa. 8.9) will continue to be written over future European history. But faith presupposes *metanoia*. This basic word of the gospel means 'Rethink!' Never was a radical change of thought more urgent than now. Are we capable of it?

Translated by John Bowden

Select bibliography

K. Bergdolt, *Der Schwarze Tod in Europa. Die große Pest und das Ende des Mittelalter*, Munich ⁵2003

F. Cardinal König and K. Rahner, *Europa. Horizonte der Hoffnung*, Graz 1983

W. Köpke and B. Schmelz (eds), *Das gemeinsame Haus Europa. Handbuch zur europäischen Kulturgeschichte. Museum für Völkerkunde Hamburg*, Munich 1999

J. Le Goff, *Die Geburt Europas im Mittelalter*, Munich 2004

R. I. Moore, *Die erste europäische Revolution. Gesellschaft und Kultur im Hochmittelalter*, Munich 2001

H. Rahner, *Abendland. Reden und Aufsätze*, Freiburg im Breisgau 1966

W. Rüegg (ed), *Geschichte der Universität in Europa* (3 vols), Munich 1993–2004

R. A. Siebenrock (ed), *Christliches Abendland – Ende oder Neuanfang?*, Theologische Trends 6, Thaur 1994

Images of Europe and Challenges of Europe for the Church: Catholicism in Recent History

ALBERTO MELLONI

Anyone who thinks that the Vatican pressure for a mention of the Christian roots of Europe in the constitution is a novelty or a fixation is mistaken: it marks the end of a long journey through history and explains how the Catholic magisterium perceives the problems posed to it by the construction of a peaceful political arena on the European continent within which work can be done.

I. The Church of Rome and the building of Europe

The interest of Roman Catholicism in the building of Europe is a constant datum in the second half of the twentieth century. When in 1948, the year in which *Pax Christi* was born, Winston Churchill convened the first European assembly in The Hague, Pius XII sent a representative to it, and Jean Monnet's idea of a Coal and Steel Community as a vehicle for broader integration found support among the Catholic leaders and diplomats of the West.[1] The creation of the Council of Europe a year later and then the adoption of the European Convention on Human Rights in 1950 was given a positive, if circumspect, response in the formation of a Catholic Secretariat for European Problems based in Strasbourg.[2] Moreover the European Defence Community, conceived of in the 1952 treaty and vetoed by a vote in the French Parliament in 1954, gained the plaudits of *La Civiltà Cattolica*,[3] the Jesuit journal which was read through in advance in the Secretariat of State. Here was the official Vatican 'yes' to an action which could open the way to a political community, predicted by the article 38 which Alcide De Gasperi wanted. Pope Pacelli, who supported the plan in his Christmas message of 1953, did not fail to give support to the treaties of Rome in 1957,[4] but the political climate and the human panorama of European governments had changed over a few years: Robert Schuman had left the Quai d'Orsay in 1953, De Gasperi died in 1954, and de-Stalinization and the invasion of Hungary made the Eastern scene more undecipherable.

Images of Europe and Challenges of Europe for the Church

Moreover, soon afterwards the pontificate of John XXIII led to a rethinking of the traditional Roman universalism in the light of the great calls for peace and decolonization which had been prepared by the congresses promoted by the mayor of Florence, Giorgio La Pira, between 1942 and 1957. In 1962 the failure of the Fouchet plan for a Europe with France and Germany as core states, and the Cuban crisis which had led the planet to the verge of nuclear obliteration,[5] called for broader approaches and checkmated the two Vatican strategies of the previous decade: its line that Christian Europe was there to safeguard Western civilization and that the continent was united against Communism[6] had proved an illusion in its view that a new regime of Christianity could guarantee peace. However, peace was becoming a concrete possibility thanks to the easing of tension and the Vatican Ostpolitik, despite the sinister appearance of the Berlin Wall.[7] Only after a decade of treaties had made the heads of European states parade before Paul VI, in 1967, did the Holy See turn towards showing concrete support for the policy of the Economic Community. The nomination in December 1970 of a nuncio to the community and a special observer to the Council of Europe indicated a direct relationship between the building of Europe and central Roman decisions. However, in the meantime the Vatican had made its proposal to the countries of the Warsaw Pact for a conference on peace and security which would see the pragmatists of Ostpolitik at work on the European scene, now conceived of as a wedge driven by wider Vatican action towards an easing of tension; it culminated in the signing of the Helsinki Treaty in 1975.[8]

II. The shift in the 1980s

This course of events, which included a serious of near breakdowns, was put in crisis when John Paul II, elected in 1978, asserted as the key feature of his geopolitical vision the rejection of the division of Europe.[9] It cannot be said for certain that previously the papacy had favoured or accepted the state of affairs created after 1947; however, it had considered the separation of the continent as a given criterion. Nor can it be said that John Paul proposed a way of overcoming the split created by the iron curtain; he simply denied its plausibility. He did so in a speech to the presiding body of the Community in 1979 and then in the course of his first visit to Poland in 1979, on which he affirmed the unity of Christian Europe – almost indicating that the long labours for a peaceful Europe, the course of which the pope had followed torn between doubts and hopes, were forms of timidity over an 'unnatural' division.[10]

The patient work done by the 120 Christian denominations (not including the Church of Rome) which in 1959 had given birth to the Conference of European Churches (CEC) by creating relationships and contacts between Christians in the political East and Christians in the political West suddenly had to measure itself against the weakness and strength of a vision. Up to that moment the CEC had been more prudent than the Catholic Church in engaging in dialogue with the Europe that was being built,[11] but it could not fail to take account of this voice from the West which spoke in the name of the East. The very assembly of presidents of the episcopal conferences of Europe which at St Gallen in 1971 had approved the Council of Episcopal Conferences of Europe (CCEE), a body which met for the first time at Chantilly in 1978,[12] appeared a poor clone of the negotiating organizations which stood for Europeanism; and as that mode of discussion gave itself tangible objectives only when elections were approaching, the Catholic Church launched a small commission (COMECE) at the time of the parliamentary elections of 1979.[13]

III. The pope's images for Europe

John Paul's speech on a single Christian Europe used powerful images to describe the way in which the Catholic Church was both becoming involved in the political community and dissociating itself from it. He mentioned the weight of the church's history,[14] the theological challenge posed by the end of the dream of Christendom,[15] the search for developed conceptual arguments,[16] and the burden of having to work out theologically the relationship between the beginning of the process of European unification and the guilt for the Second World War and the Shoah.[17] However, it is the images which impress themselves on one's mind, in a series connected with the development of the history of the Union, but also influencing each other. Although we still await an *Enchiridion Europae*, which is perhaps rendered superfluous by the availability of the pope's speeches on the internet, it is possible to mention some of the most important.

Among them the recurrence of 'Christian Europe', the term used at Gniezno in 1979, has a basic function. It draws on the myth of Christendom elaborated in conservative Catholic theology which was taken up again in the Catholic culture of the 1930s: this dream of a Christendom postulates, over against modernity, the 'ideal' model of a society which finds prosperity and peace in obediently receiving the basic principles of life from the church authorities. Dear to the leaders of the Catholic parties of post-war Europe,[18] this myth did not bring salvation from the experience of secularization and had in fact been overtaken by the experiences and ecclesiological conceptions of Vatican II.[19] It is not clear what application the idea of a past Christian Europe has except in one respect, namely the impossibility of identifying the church with the West. Simply in political terms, more upbeat over the recent past in its opposition to Communism,[20] Wojtyla's church does not feel obliged to have a privileged relationship with the United States, though for various reasons this was indispensable for the Fanar.[21]

In 1987, in the encyclical *Redemptoris Mater*, John Paul began to make frequent use of another image, that of the 'two lungs'. It had been coined by Vjaceslav Ivanov, a Russian poet living in Rome between 1924 and 1949, who had produced the image of one church, destined physiologically to breathe with a Western lung and an Eastern lung from which it had been separated for too long.[22] When linked to the confessional division of the church and made the vehicle of an ecumenical message, this image took on a new political significance, indicating not so much (or not only) the construction of a common political space in Europe as the overcoming of the division into blocs.

This is a destiny which is also linked up with the expression, used by De Gaulle, of the extension of Europe, namely 'from the Atlantic to the Urals'. John Paul II used the phrase in his speech at Spira on 4 May 1987; the formula, which De Gaulle saw as compensating for the bias towards the Atlantic in European politics, appeared in the pope's speech after the failure of the project of a European Union at the Community's assembly in February 1984 had led the way to the creation of a common market and sanctioned the priority of the economic project over the political project. For the pope it corresponded to a European vocation to gain the dimensions destined 'by geography and even more by history', as he told the European Parliament on 11 October 1988.

Among the images used in Catholic discourse we also find the formula pioneered in Bonn by Leonid Brezhnev in 1981, of the 'common European house', in which peace and security were guaranteed along the lines of stability fixed in Helsinki. This became part of the pontifical magisterium, an instrument in the dialogue with Mikhail Gorbachev, and above all the cipher for a Europe in which union was only one of many possibilities.

This kaleidoscope of images in fact indicates that rather than entertaining the prospect of 'union' (the formula is that of Pompidou in 1972), the Rome of Pope Wojtyla was thinking of the need to overcome the split caused by the Cold War and to restore dialogue between peoples and nations, and then waiting to see how and when the political framework would change. This was not unprecedented caution: the peaceful return of Portugal, Greece and Spain to democracy in the middle of the 1970s had not had immediate repercussions on the way in which the Holy See regarded Europe and its divisions; so the democratization of the East heralded by the Polish revolution sparked off by Solidarity did not indicate to the church the need to make a more direct contribution than producing a term of reference.

Over and above the recommendations made by the pope in his visits and on important European anniversaries,[23] the first programmatic statement within the life of European Catholicism was that made on the Youth Day at Compostela in August 1988; this was the slogan of a 'new evangelization'. Conceived of on the eve of the Soviet collapse, this vision, not of Europe but of its needs, became a leitmotif of Catholic preaching, with obvious weaknesses and contradictions.[24] However, in a European framework it has a more marked significance since, notwithstanding the major commitment in the ecumenical appointments from Basle onwards, it is evident that this formula does not leave room to recognize in the peaceful process which had brought the cold war to an end, and on the contrary proposed a Catholicism in a permanent state of mobilization, a therapy for a continent afflicted by secularity.

IV. The battle over roots

From the moment when the constitutional process in the EU came to life, between the Maastricht Treaty of 1992 and the Charter of Nice in 2001,[25] a new image was used widely in communications to the public, that of 'roots'. Whereas in a first phase the pope had raised the problem whether God should be mentioned in the foundation document of European society (something which would also be dear to Lutheran theology),[26] from 2000 the expression 'Christian roots' or 'Judaeo-Christian roots' was coined as a litmus test for the receptiveness of countries, parties and politics to the fully legitimate authority of the Holy See, an authority which was asserted progressively until the end of 2003.[27]

Judgments on the content and form of these pleas have not been unanimous. For many, the mention of a Christian heritage (*sic et simpliciter*) was a truism rather than a cause of war: and it is difficult to say that in a list of traditions which Thucydides did not leave out, one has to jump over Greek, Latin Arab and Slavonic Christianity. Others, however, had noted with good reason that the demand that Europe and Christianity should be superimposed in the constitution of Europe would end up in the revival of a myth all too burdened with traditional Christian antisemitism. This led to talk of Jewish-Christian roots, but with a hyphen that caused even more alarm, because it presupposed the absorption of one term in the other, precisely as in the substitutionary theology of classical antisemitism. That was certainly not the intention of the Catholic magisterium (this formula is used in the speeches of John Paul II and in the apostolic exhortation *Ecclesia in Europa* of June 2003); however, it became evident that a formula indicating different identities should have said 'Jewish and Christian' – and that did injustice to the long presence of Islam on the Iberian peninsula, in Sicily and the Balkans, the exclusion of which could not be justified.

It is not easy to get out of this labyrinth, but no one was forced to enter it. At one moment (a concern of Mgr Migliore, then in the Secretary of State[28]) it seemed that the major preoccupation for the Vatican was the stability of the 1929 Lateran Treaty, which some thought should be guaranteed by a European concordat. More generally there were many themes – options on war, freedom of conscience,[29] religious rights[30] and the prospect of inter-religious integration,[31] the rethinking of the secular character of the state[32] – about which Catholics were very anxious during the debate on Giscard's convention. However, after accepting with concealed satisfaction the principle of 'unstructured' dialogue between the religions and Europe,[33] the Catholic Church ceased to insist that the formula of 'roots' should be constitutionalized, thus ceasing to promote its own improbable causes.

V. The Europe of religious co-existence

The outcome of the Vatican pressure on the drafting of the text of the Constitution[34] is still uncertain and in any case exposed to occasional crises (like that over the veil in France, which gives Islamic fundamentalism an easy cause and stirs people up over the principle of laicity).[35] However, the discussion on roots has itself shown how the process of the union, expansion and constitutionalization of Europe poses new problems to all religions, to the churches, and also to Roman Catholicism, as they all address the future.

A Europe constructed of states with the benevolent neutrality of the churches has in fact created a completely new situation of cohabitation. This differs from the cohabitation of the Ottoman empire, which revolved around inequality, and from the systems of tolerance and secularity in modern Europe, which regulated the peaceful coexistence of a very limited number of subjects; it also differs from the American separatist model bound up with a sense of civil religion anchored in the generic figure of God. By contrast, Europe is revealed as the place where faiths, agnosticisms and atheisms which over the centuries have grown up in separate spaces co-exist and are now unexpectedly exposed to one another's demands and distrust, outside the framework of ecumenism or inter-religious dialogue.[36] So the Catholic course must be measured up to a more cautious Orthodoxy,[37] which for example sees the possible inclusion of Turkey in the European Union as a strategic preoccupation, one that raises a question about the status of the ecumenical patriarch which is not shared with the others; the traditional Protestant distrust of Europeanism is bound up with a more mature structure of representation.[38]

VI. The EU and Catholicism

The topic of the EU opens up complex questions not only in the relationship between the churches but also within the churches. The Catholic Church faces three such issues, all of which are very delicate.

In the first place Catholicism has the problem of relating the role of the Holy See to that of its episcopal bodies. A contradiction which has already been experienced at the national level in Italy is here experienced at the European level; in Italy, where the pope is primate, papal diplomacy has negotiated the public status of the episcopal conference in concordats; where the pope is primate, the conference is to a lesser degree the protagonist, so as not to put the papacy in the shade. On the European scale this dilemma has still to be resolved. If the episcopal conferences of the EU established a single conference with a president (elected, as everywhere else, or nominated by the pope, as in Italy?), Roman ecclesiastical government would have to rethink its own role and function completely. It is unthinkable that the decisions taken by an episcopal assembly with twice as many members as the Council of Trent could be scrutinized or invalidated by the consultants to the Congregations of the Roman Curia as they are today, or that in the name of the bishop this body should remain without a voice in the capital. On the other hand a conference which limited itself to going it alone or lobbying around the pontifical magisterium would end up by impoverishing the authority and the testimony of the church.

Secondly, the Petrine function, forced by the new history of the Union to express itself in the same political space in which the voices of the patriarchs, the communions and the church federations are heard, would have to find new registers of Catholicism. This universality which Vatican I thought of in terms of jurisdiction now becomes a spiritual and cultural need, in order to prevent the papacy, and with it Catholicism, once again finding themselves imprisoned by a European hegemony. The pluralism of the church of which Vatican II was the manifestation and which was confirmed by the travels of John Paul II underlines this; it is clear that the church can no longer be limited to a European perspective and a European mentality.[39]

Conversely, the synods on the continent – held under John Paul II in a form which is still humiliating to the dignity of the bishops - must respond to the challenge of European models of decision-making, by responsible and adult individuals. A lack of this was felt – to give an example – when John Paul II's opposition to the war in Iraq was not supported by any worthwhile voice from the European episcopate as a dialogue partner, but only in an *ad hoc* way.

Talk of the Christian roots of Europe in the future constitution is thus only one element in a great mosaic of problems; whether or not it will have any impact on the framework within which the rethinking of Europe is taking place remains to be seen.

Translated by John Bowden

Notes

1. Cf. G. Audisio, *I fondatori dell'Europa unita secondo il progetto di Jean Monnet: Robert Schuman, Konrad Adenauer, Alcide De Gasperi*, Cantalupa 1999; D. Preda, *Sulla soglia dell'Unione. La vicenda della Comunità politica europea (1952–1954)*, Milan 1999.
2. C. De Montclos, 'Le Saint-Siège et la construction de l'Europe' in J.-B. D'Onorio (ed), *Le Vatican et la politique européenne*, Paris 1994, pp. 85–105.
3. E. Di Nolfo, 'La Civiltà Cattolica e le scelte di fondo della politica estera italiana nel secondo dopoguerra' in *Storia e politica*, Milan 1971, pp. 187ff.
4. P. Chenaux, *Une Europe Vaticane? Entre le Plan Marshall et les Traités de Rome*, Brussels 1990.
5. Cf. A. Melloni, *L'altra Roma. Politica e S. Sede durante il concilio Vaticano II (1959–1965)*, Bologna 2000.
6. Chenaux, *Une Europe Vaticane?* (n. 4), pp. 277–84.
7. Cf. A. Riccardi, 'Antisovietismo e Ostpolitk della santa Sede da Benedetto XV a Paolo VI' in *Un diplomatico vaticano fra dopoguerra e Ostpolitik. Mons. Mario Cagna (1911–1986)* ed A. Melloni and M. Guasco, Bologna 2003, pp. 217–42.
8. *CSCE: From Idea to Institution. A Bibliography* ed H. Holtermann, Copenhagen 1993; A. Carrascosa Coso, *La Santa Sede y la conferencia sobre la seguridad y la cooperacion en Europa*, Cuenca 1990.
9. The speeches of John Paul II can be found by date in the volumes of *Insegnamenti* or at vatican.va.
10. A. Riccardi, *Governo carismatico, 25 anni di pontificato*, Milano 2003.
11. Only in 1989 did the CEC engage in dialogue with the European Commission.
12. C. Thiede, *Bischöfe-kollegial für Europa. CCEE im Dienst einer sozialetisch konkretisierten Evangelisierung*, Ms 1991.

13. From 1976 on there was an information service for Catholic Europe which after 1979, with Vatican support, became COMECE and acted as an interface between the Catholics present in the Assembly (the main appointments are in *Lexikon für Theologie und Kirche* s.v. 'Europa/Kirchliche Strukturen').
14. I have discussed this in my 'L'Europa delle religioni', *Il Mulino* 51/6, 2002, no. 404, pp. 1057–66.
15. *Das neue Europa. Herausforderung für Kirche und Theologie* ed P. Hünermann, Freiburg im Breisgau 1993.
16. E.g. by J. Ratzinger, *Christliche Glaube und Europa*, Munich 1981; id., *Wendezeit für Europa? Diagnosen und Prognosen zur Lage von Kirche und Welt*, Freiburg im Breisgau 1991.
17. D. Dietrich, *God and Humanity in Auschwitz: Jewish-Christian Relations and Sanctioned Murder*, New Brunswick 1995.
18. A. Giovagnoli, *Le premesse della ricostruzione: tradizione e modernità nella classe dirigente del dopoguerra*, Milan 1982; P. Scoppola and F. Traniello (eds), *I cattolici tra fascismo e democrazia*, Bologna 1975; G. R. Horn (ed), *Left Catholicism: Catholics and Society in Western Europe at the Point of Liberation, 1943–1955*, Leuven 2001.
19. G. Bottoni (ed), *Fine della cristianità? Il cristianesimo tra religione civile e testimonianza evangelica*, Bologna 2002.
20. Cf. A. Riccardi, *Il Vaticano e Mosca 1940–1990*, Rome and Bari 1992.
21. For the election of Athenagoras as patriarch and his line cf. E. Di Nolfo, *Il Vaticano e gli Stati Uniti. Dalle carte di Myron Taylor*, Milan 1978; V. Martano, *Athenagoras il patriarca (1886–1972). Un cristiano fra crisi della coabitazione e utopia ecumenica*, Bologna 1996.
22. For him see the proceedings of the congress on Russia and Europa (Rome, 28 October-1 November 2001). For Europe as reflected by the first Russian emigration see Vjaceslav Ivanov, *Poesia e sacra scrittura*.
23. According to De Montclos, 'Le Saint-Siège et la construction de l'Europe' (n. 2), pp. 96–9, the Roman directives of the 1990s turn on four points: the refusal to reduce citizens to consumers, mistrust of the use of individual freedom, criticism of the dominant social model, and respect for national identities.
24. Cf. R. Luneau (ed), *Le rêve de Compostelle. Vers la restauration d'une Europe chrétienne?*, Paris 1989.
25. For the attempt to draw up a European constitution within the framework of the European Defence Commuity cf. N. Antonetti, 'I progetti costituzionali europei: caratteri storici e istituzionali (1953–1994)', and L. Violini, 'La Costituzione europea fra passato e presente' in *Costituzionalizzare l'Europa ieri ed oggi* ed U. De Siervo, Bologna 2001, pp. 23–70 and 71–104.
26. For the idea of an appeal to divine law as the foundation of different political solutions in Grozio cf. J.-L. Blaquart, 'Le politique et le religieux dans l'évolution de l'Europe: une histoire plurielle, un avenir commun?', *Revue d'éthique et de théologie morale, Le Supplément* (2003), no. 226, pp. 7–13, and various other

references in the fascicle dedicated to *Degré de modernité des états en Europe*, ed J.-P. Durand.
27. For the barrage of papal speeches to the European ambassadors to the Holy See cf. DC 85, 2003, 2283.
28. The request was put forward by Mgr Migliore in the colloquium on 'The Situation of the Churches and the Religious Communities of the EU and the Obligations of Member States Presente and Future', held in Perugia from 21–23 March 2002, promoted by G. Barberini. Cf. F. Margiotta Broglio, 'Ancora sulle origini dell'art. 7 della Costituzione: un progetto di Jacques Maritain per l'internazionalizzazione dei Patti Laternanesi e propositi della Santa Sede per l'ampliamento della Città del Vaticano (1944–1948)' in *Studi in onore di Lorenzo Spinelli*, I, Modena 1989, pp. 851–66.
29. 'Conscience oblige. Entretien avec Claude Geffré' in *La tolérance. Pour une humanisme hérétique* ed C. Sahel, Paris 1993, pp. 55–70.
30. Cf. S. Ferrari and I. C. Ibán, *Diritto e religione in Europa occidentale*, Bologna 1997; A. Canavero and J.-D. Durand, *Il fattore religioso nell'integrazione europea*, Milan 1999.
31. J. Doré (ed), *Le christianisme vis-à-vis des religions*, Namur 1997; F. Boespflug, *Assise, dix ans après*, Paris 1996.
32. This is the thesis of E. Poulat, *Liberté - Laîcité. La guerre des deux France et le principe del modernité*, Paris; id. *La solution laïque et ses problemes*, Paris 1997.
33. In 1978 a group of European laymen (Philip, Rey and the Swiss philosopher de Rougemont) created a body for Anglican-Protestant representation in Brussels, the European Ecumenical Commission for Church and Society (EECCS). This was moved to Strasbourg in 1986, and in 1990 the EECCS had a 'structured dialogue' with the Commission which put forward requests from all the churches.
34. Cf. *Valéry Giscard d'Estaing présente La Constitution pour l'Europe*, Maurice Schuman Foundation, Paris 2003.
35. For the regression of the holy war see the optimism of G. Kepel, *Jihad: expansion et déclin de l'islamisme*, Paris 2000. *Islamic fundamentalism* ed Abdel Salam Sidahmed and Anoushiravan Ehteshami, Boulder, CO 1996.
36. The ecumenical organisms do not serve this purpose; only in 1999 did the WCC in Geneva open a European desk. For the dialogue cf. G. Ruggieri, 'Pluralismo religioso: da motivo di conflitto a speranza di pace' in *Conflitti violenza pace: sfida alle religioni. Atti della XXXVII Sessione di formazione ecumenica. Chianciano Terme, 22–29 luglio 2000*, edited by the Segretariato Attività ecumeniche, Milan 2001, pp. 23–40.
37. Only from 2000 did Admantios of Reghion represent the Ecumenical Patriarch of Constantinople at the Commission; with the entry of Turkey into the Union this broke 550 years of isolation. In 2002 the Patriarchate of Moscow transferred Metropolitan Ilarion Alfeev from England to Brussels as delegate of the Patriarch of Moscow. Cf. V. Makrdides, 'Le rôle de l'orthodoxie dans la

formation de l'antieuropéanisme et l'antioccidentalisme grecs' in G. Vincent and J.-P. Willaime, *Religions et transformations de l'Europe*, Strasbourg 1993, pp. 103–16.

38. From 1948 to 1969 the EKD also represented East Germany; in the World Council of Churches a group presided over by André Philip, head of the French delegation to the WCC from 1949 to 1951, worked on a document on 'The Christian Responsibility in European Collaboration' (1950); this did not overcome the mistrust of Orthodox and Protestants. Cf. F. G. Dreyfus, 'Le protestantisme contre l'Europe' in Vincent and Willaime, *Religions et transformations de l'Europe* (n. 37), pp. 127–41.

39. The dissent developing in the Anglican Communion over the ordination of homosexuals to the episcopate deserves a thorough study.

The 'New' Europe: A Spiritual Gesture

ERIK BORGMAN

The central hypothesis of this article is that there is a spiritual and religious aspect in the European identity. But although especially Catholics and their organizations tend to stress the Christian origin of Europe, and although in the 1950s founding fathers Konrad Adenhauer (Germany), Alcide De Gaspari (Italy) and Robert Schuman (France) were Catholics, although the formation treaty for the European Economic Community in 1957 was signed in Rome and the signatories visited Pope Pius XII, and although there were strong speculations about the new Europe being a resurrection of the Holy Roman Empire, modern Europe is a secular project. The religious significance of modern Europe is to be found in its very secularity. It might be a good thing to include the word 'God' in the future European constitution, as some are defending, but not as a memento to the religious origin of values that were secularized later on in the European cultures. Rather, to make reference to God means to acknowledge that every human project is a response to an opportunity that was first given, and that whatever is realized never equals what should be realized. The word 'God' is a memento to the fact that no culture ever realizes the truly good life, but that we may always hope for new opportunities to further humanization.

I. The mission to make missions obsolete

Recently, in the discussion on the after September 11 strategy to stop terrorism and on the legitimacy of starting a pre-emptive war in Iraq, the spiritual identity of Europe unexpectedly became an issue. In analogy with a stereotypical view on gender differences, summarized in the book title *Men are from Mars, Women are from Venus*, American political analyst Robert Kagan stated that Americans are from Mars and Europeans are from Venus.[1] Gender stereotypes aside, Kagan feels that, whereas in his view Americans are fully conscious of the fact that they live in the world Thomas Hobbes described as consisting of a war of all against all in which only power and violence can impose some order, Europeans on their own continent live

Immanuel Kant's vision of perpetual peace in which power is balanced by right, and enlightened self-interest constrains the tendency to irrational goals and the use of excessive force to reach them. On the one hand, Kagan suggests that Europe's strategy is a realistic one for a militarily weak continent. On the other hand, he claims that through becoming accustomed to relative peace, Europe has lost sight of the fact that its own tranquillity is still exceptional. The law of the jungle prevails everywhere else.

What Kagan and like-minded colleagues seem to forget is that Europe's strategy in international affairs came into existence as an answer to a Hobbesian world of uncontrollable and recurring violence. The Europe constructed since the late 1940s is an attempt to constrain violence through shared interest and concrete solidarity between former enemies. The revolutionary spiritual discovery of the new Europe lies in its implicit awareness that it has arisen from the ruins of a cluster of ideologies: fascism and anti-semitism, communism and anti-communism. The new Europe that first took shape in 1952 with the formation of the European Coal and Steel Community was born from the experience that 'all who take the sword will perish by the sword' (Matt. 26.52). Avoiding violence is in everyone's interest, and that the best way to avoid it is to make it a less viable option.

The origins of European Union as we know it today were thus pragmatic through and through and at every stage. There was never a master plan that just needed to be implemented; rather, opportunities to enhance integration were seized when they presented themselves. New agreements and new treaties created new facts and situations, and with each development discussion then proceeded what the next step might be.[2] Recently there have been complaints that Europe lacks a long-term vision, a clear awareness of its internal and external mission. Former president of the European Commission Jacques Delors has stated repeatedly and eloquently that we have 'to give a soul to Europe, to give it spirituality and meaning'. Although Delors has a point, it should equally be acknowledged that the European Community is the outcome of a process which began with the abandonment of utopian visions that needed violence to implement them. The whole point of the new Europe was to make militant missions obsolete by establishing formal decision-making processes and bureaucracies. . If Europe has a soul, a spirituality and a meaning, as I think it does, it is one enshrined in this pragmatic approach.

II. Solidarity in destiny

Ironically, a fine example of what I take to be an archetypically new-European act was done by an American in the summer of 1993. Bosnia in former Yugoslavia was a war zone and Sarajevo under siege when the American writer, literary critic and director Susan Sontag staged there a production of Samuel Becket's *Waiting for Godot* with local actors. It became a liturgical happening, in the way of a classical Greek tragedy. The despair and the fear of the people of Sarajevo, their feeling of being lost and left alone, were expressed and represented by the actors playing Vladimir and Estragon in their endless wait for the mysterious Godot, always coming but never arriving.

Looking back, Sontag wrote:

> I think it was at the end of the [third] performance – on Wednesday, August 18 at 2:00 pm – during the long tragic silence of the Vladimirs and the Estragons [Sontag had split Becket's central personages in different roles, in order to make it possible for more actors to be in the play; EB] which follows the messenger's announcement that Mr Godot isn't coming today, but will certainly come tomorrow, that my eyes began to sting with tears. Velibor [one of the actors; EB] was crying, too. No one in the public made a sound.[3]

In Sarajevo, *Waiting for Godot* created the strange but real consolation of being inconsolable together, of holding on together to waiting for true consolation and of realizing that, while waiting together with others, one is not absolutely forsaken in the midst of forsakenness. In my view this is closely akin to what the Christian tradition expresses on Good Friday and to its belief that Jesus Christ, 'though he was in the form of God, did not count equality with God a thing to be grasped, but emptied himself . . . being born in the likeness of humans . . ., [and] humbled himself and became obedient unto death, even death on a cross' (Phil. 2.6–8). Not being alone in forlornness signifies a life beyond forlornness. Solidarity with people threatened by violence to the point of death on a cross, is the ultimate expression of hope for this world filled with crosses.[4]

Although the public attention focussed almost exclusively on its military aspect, it was especially from a spiritual point of view that the wars in former Yugoslavia were a major test for the European Union. The Union failed the test, not so much because it was unable to stop the violence and needed America once again to clear up its mess – as the Americans and many leading European commentators came to see it afterwards – but because it did not treat the killings, the deportations and the mass murders as its own problems, as questions it had to answer, as a situation in which it was inescapably involved. This was a spiritual failure as much as anything else.

For a brief period of time the Dutch government was an exception. In 1994, it sent a battalion to defend Srebrenica in Bosnia, declared a Safe Area by the United Nations peacekeeping forces. During the events leading eventually to the fall of the enclave in July 1995, the idea of – in Dutch – '*lotsverbondenheid*' ('solidarity in destiny') became the semi-official term to indicate the basic principle of Dutch policy in Srebrenica. 'Solidarity in destiny' qualifies, I think, as a rather accurate expression of the 'soul' of post-World War II Europe at its best. However, the effectiveness of this principle in this situation was limited. On 11 July 1995 the Dutch government officially stated the solidarity of the Dutch unit known as *Dutchbat* with the destiny of the Muslims of Srebrenica. They were besieged together by the Serbs and the Dutch military forces agreed to stay in their uncertain situation as long as the destiny of the Muslims was uncertain. However, on 13 July *Dutchbat* sent away the Muslims who had sought protection in their compound and left Srebrenica in order to save itself, fully aware that the lives of especially the Muslim men and boys were in danger. Thousands of them would indeed be killed.

There was then an intensive discussion in the Netherlands on what went wrong and who was to blame, In April 2002, after an official report on the affair was published, the Dutch government fell because of 'Srebrenica'. However, the three volume and almost 3,400 page report focussed on the question whether the troops should have been sent to the enclave in the first place. What went wrong in the decision-making process and how could similar situations be avoided in the future?[5] The lesson drawn was to be more careful not to send Dutch troops to situations in which their mission and their mandate are unclear. In fact, this means forfeiting the principle of 'solidarity in destiny', where outcomes are by definition unclear.

III. Economic development: from the means to the end

It is still possible to understand the recent history of Europe as a gradual discovery of the necessity and implications of the idea of 'solidarity in destiny', however flawed this has been in practice. The European Community was established among the ruins of World War II by joint acceptance of the ruinous economical, political and even moral situation as a collective inheritance.

This is not to deny that self-interest was also a strongly motivating force. There might never have been a European Community had the American Secretary of State George Marshall in 1947 not offered the European countries 13 billion dollars worth of aid on the condition that they plan their economic recovery together. This obliged the sixteen countries in 1948 to form the Organization for Economic European Co-operation which would later become the Organization for Economic Co-operation and Development, and obliged the nations within it to make each other's problems their own concern.

Anti-communism and the will to win the competition with Eastern Europe were equally important motivations for the countries with a capitalist economy to join forces. However, between 1945 and 1989 there was also a growing awareness that the division of Europe into two camps was itself part of the common and unsatisfactory situation for which all European peoples had to take responsibility. *Détente* in the 1970s,[6] Western-European protests against nuclear arms in the early 1980s[7] and the advocacy of values of a Civil Society amongst the leaders' opposition groups in Central Europe in the later 1980s[8] – these were all aspects of a growing belief that Europe should have a common future.

All this is not to deny that the European countries developed their solidarity by excluding others from the benefits it produced. This, if no other reason, makes it an exaggeration to see European history since 1945 as an ongoing development of Europe as a project to let unity be born from diversity, plurality and conflicts.[9] What we have seen is a series of opportunities to discover Europe as such a project. There are and will be new opportunities, from which there can come new insights. Europe does not even now understand itself explicitly in terms of a shared vision of a future that is at present hidden in the diverse but related histories of its countries.

And this is not coincidental but closely related to the foundation mythology of Western civilization – just as, according to Greek mythology, order was established by forcefully taming the violent powers of chaos personified by the Titans, so Western culture tends to see itself as forcing stability on the chaotic violence of nature. Establishing civilization means defeating the natural tendencies that work counter to it, and containing them within their proper limits. Just as technology is imagined as taming nature in the strict sense of the word, government is imagined as the art of keeping the 'natural' inclinations of people towards greed and hatred, selfishness and violence to others within limits. Or better still: good government is considered to be the art of using these inclinations, which left to themselves tend to lead to discord and conflict, for the benefit of all. This is what the economy does, according to a tradition that starts with Adam Smith's *Wealth of Nations* (1775) and builds on the phrase in Bernard Mandeville's *Fable of the Bees* (1714); private vices can be made into public benefits.

Starting in the seventeenth century, spiritual and religious convictions came to be seen as subjective, arbitrary, based on instinct and emotion, and therefore tending to violence. There was always the danger of stirring up emotions which might lead to violent clashes, as the wars of religion of the sixteenth century had made obvious according to the most influential European political thinkers. In our own day the threat of 'fundamentalism' works as a public reminder that this possibility is still present. In other words, the famous principle of separation of church and state, which became canonized after the French Revolution and is commonly considered to be at the core of modern Western civilization, is based on the idea that religion is less a civilizing than a principally de-stabilizing and chaotic, potentially violent force.[10] This semi-religious claim that secularized society is the redemption of human beings from the arbitrariness, authoritarianism and violence of religion, is transposed to the economy and leads the political eagerness to rely on the economical powers to develop discipline and appeasement, notwithstanding the clearly violent nature of many economic developments.[11]

IV. Religious dedication to vulnerability

But every understanding of a situation and of what should be done in response to it involves at least an implicit view on the totality of which it is part. These horizons are what religions and other so-called philosophies of life provide. In a pluralistic society such views are never shared by all, and there are good political as well as theological reasons not to try to change that. Nevertheless it is impossible to make abstraction of one's own view, and there are good reasons to suggest that it is politically and theologically undesirable too to try to change that. According to the so-called Böckenförde-dilemma it is impossible democratically to guarantee the values on which democracy is founded.[12] Therefore, democracy depends on the rationales for it and the visions on it provided by the different religious and philosophical traditions present in it, but not founded by or through it. This should lead Europe to, I think, giving up the attempt to escape from religion into secularity, and admitting that we inescapably live in a situation of discussion, struggle and sometimes conflict between different religions or traditions of interpretation in religions.

This does not mean surrendering to chaos and irrationality, but trusting in the tendencies towards rationality and the tools for conflict-solving within religion. As the German theologian Jürgen Manemann has pointed out, it is a mistake simply to interpret the violence that destroyed the Twin Towers in New York on September 11 2001 as just an expression of 'religious mania', as did the German newsmagazine *Der Spiegel*. Rather and in spite of the religious rhetoric used to justify it, in its very nihilism, its hatred of everything that there is and exists, its joy in destruction and annihilation, September 11 expressed an *irreligious* mania. It is a mania born from the lack of the typical religious reference for everything that is gifted with being, for the gift of being itself and therefore in the end of the Giver of being.[13] Religions may have the tendency to become overzealous in preaching and enforcing their truths and are to that extent always in danger of becoming violent, but they are also characterized by an inherent reserve against the nihilistic aspect of violence. In this light, it is possible to interpret the recent history of Europe as other than a history of secularization and liberation from religion. The historic attempt Europe made over the last decades to overcome violence by strengthening the multilateral solidarity in destiny can itself be read as a religious history, and it seems theologically important and politically wise to do so.

What Europe discovered in the second half of the twentieth century is that there is no alternative to democracy. There is no changing of the cultural and political reality but from the inside, by the people involved. Other approaches are inherently violent and lead to violence. We are unavoidably involved in each other's destiny, and the only viable way to change our destiny goes through being in solidarity with the destiny of one another. However, as the German philosopher Helmut Dubiel puts it, democracy is 'the institutionalized form of dealing publicly with uncertainty' and a 'posttraditional civil religion'.[14] Its core religious and spiritual value is 'weakness', not in the sense of not knowing what to say, what to do or what to feel, but in the sense of solidarity in the human destiny of being vulnerable.

This needs to be expressed in something like the 'weak' theology the Dominican friar and theologian Ulrich Engel found necessary to uphold forcefully, given the worldwide state of war we are living in since September 11 2001.[15] From a Christian point of view, this 'weak' theology mirrors the image of God as closely related to our histories of weakness and vulnerability. For me, this is the God who should be mentioned in the future European constitution. Not as the God of the Christians and their tradition – although I think that the Christian tradition is focussed on the expression of reference to this God – but as the always hidden divine presence in our necessarily weak and vulnerable attempts to realize something of a good life against all odds, a counter to our desire to change history with one violent and final gesture.

I do not think that this God will in fact be mentioned in the constitution that is being constructed, but I do think that our remembrance and the awareness of this God constitutes to a large degree the future of Europe and the future of the world.

Notes

1. Robert Kagan, 'Power and Weakness', *Polity Review* June 2002; id., *Of Paradise and Power: America and Europe in the New World Order*, New York: Knopf 2003. Cf. John Gray, *Men are from Mars, Women are from Venus: A Practical Guide for Improving Communication and Getting What You Want in Your Relationship*, London: Thorsons 1997.
2. For accounts of the history of the European unification, cf. Alan S. Milward, *The European Rescue of the Nation-State*, Berkeley: University of California Press 1992; A. Moravcsik, *The Choice for Europe: Social Purpose and State Power from Messina to Maastricht*, Ithaca: Cornell University Press 1998.
3. Susan Sontag, 'Waiting for Godot in Sarajevo' in *Where the Stress Falls: Essays*, London: Jonathan Cape 2002, pp. 299–322: 322.
4. Cf. David Toole, *Waiting for Godot in Sarajevo: Theological Reflections on Nihilism, Tragedy, and Apocalypse*, London: SCM Press 2001 (1998).
5. Nederlands Instituut voor Oorlogsdocumentatie, *Srebrenica, een veilig gebied: Reconstructie, achtergronden, gevolgen en analyses van de val van een Safe Area*, Amsterdam: Boom 2002
6. Cf. Wilfried Loth, *Overcoming the Cold War: A History of Détente, 1950–1991*, Basingstoke: Palgrave 2002.
7. Cf. Harald Müller (ed), *Europe and Nuclear Disarmament: Debates and Political Attitutes in 16 European Countries*, Brussels: European Interuniversity Press 1998.
8. Cf. for instance György Konrád, *Antipolitik: Mitteleuropäische Meditiationen*, Frankfurt am Main: Suhrkamp 1985 (1984); Adam Michnik, *Letters from Prison and other Essays*, Berkely/Los Angeles: University of California Press 1985; Jan Vladislav (ed), *Václav Havel, or Living in Truth: Twenty-two Essays Published on the Occasion of the Award of the Erasmus Prize to Václav Havel*, Amsterdam: Meulenhof 1986; see also: Václav Havel, *Toward a Civil Society: Selected Speeches and Writings 1990–1994*, Pargue: Lidové Noviny 1995.
9. This is the point of M. Heirman, *De ontdekking van Europa: Een geschiedenis van de toekomst*, Antwerpen: Houtekiet 2003.
10. Cf. John Milbank, *Theology and Social Theory: Beyond Secular Reason*, Oxford: Blackwell 1990, pp. 9–27; William T. Cavanaugh, *Theopolitical Imagination: Discovering the Liturgy as a Political Act in an Age of Global Consumerism*, London/New York: T. & T. Clark, 2002, pp.15–31.

11. This suggests that market economics is itself best understood as a religion, as is the thesis of Robert H. Nelson, *Economics as Religion: From Samuelson to Chicago and Beyond*, Univerity Park: Penn State Press 2001.
12. Ernst-Wolfgang Böckenförde, *Recht, Staat, Freiheit: Studien zur Rechtphilosophie, Staatstheorie und Verfassungsgeschichte*, Frankfurt am Main 1991, 112 (ET *State, Society and Liberty: Studies in Political Theory and Constitutional Law*, New York: Berg 1991).
13. Jürgen Manemann, 'Religiöser Wahn oder Wahnsinn aus Irreligiosität?', *Orientierung* 65 (2001) 213–214; cf. *Der Spiegel* 55 (2001) no. 41, entitled: 'Der religiöse Wahn: Die Rückkehre des Mittelalters'.
14. Helmut Dubiel, *Ungewißheit und Politik*, Frankfurt am Main: Suhrkamp 1994, especially pp.178–185; cf. Johann Baptist Metz, *Zum Begriff der neuen Politischen Theologie 1967–1997*, l.c., pp. 174–196: 'Religion und Poltik an den Grenzen der Moderne: Versuch einer Neubestimmung'.
15. Ulrich Engel, 'Religion and Violence: Plea for a "Weak" Theology *In Tempore Belli*', *New Blackfriars* 82 (2001), pp.558–60.

From Tolerance to Rights: Religions in the Unification Process

SILVIO FERRARI

I. Introduction

The recipe for writing a good constitution contains two basic ingredients. First of all it is necessary to have a correct reading of the social and political realities which are to be translated into norms: the constitution must respect the traditions, convictions and values on which the co-existence of a social community is based. Secondly it must have the capacity to offer a perspective on the present: a constitution must be capable of awakening hopes, of indicating objectives and a way of reaching them. A constitution which is only a photograph of reality is old the moment it is born; it also has to contain a genetic code capable of prefiguring and accompanying the growth of a national or super-national community, which is what the European Community is.

These observations also apply to the current debate on religion in the future constitution of the European Union. We can only start from the present, so the first part of this article is devoted to a short description of relationships between states and religions in the countries of the European Union. However, at the same time we have to orientate ourselves on the future, so the next part will evaluate the possibilities of development contained in these models of relationships. I shall conclude the article with some reflections on the draft constitution which has emerged from the work of the European Convention and on the impact that this may have in defining future relations between states and religions in the European Union.

II. A European model of relations between states and religions?

At first glance the national systems of relations between states and religions give the impression of being extremely diverse. There are few similarities between Denmark with a state church and a separatist and secular France, or between the system of recognized religions which has been adopted in

Belgium and that current in Greece, based on the predominance of a single religion.

In reality this first impression is superficial, and stops at the superstructures of the legal system. We only have to go a little deeper to see that there are some shared principles which make it possible to make out a common model of relationships between states and religions.[1]

The first of these principles is the freedom and religious equality of individuals, i.e. the right to have, not to have, to change and to practise one's own religion publicly. This is a principle which has ancient roots, but in its present form it is affirmed through the philosophical reflections of the Enlightenment and the work of the liberal nineteenth-century jurists. It therefore presents itself as a key principle of modernity: every human being, simply by virtue of being human, has the right to make in absolute freedom choices in keeping with conscience, without being subjected to any discrimination in relation to those choices. It would be excessive to say that this principle is respected all over Europe: there are countries – Greece, where proselytization is forbidden, but also France, where there is a desire to forbid Muslim women students to wear the veil – which limit more or less markedly the right to practise one's own religion publicly. However, it is a fact that today, in all the countries of the European Union, Catholics, Protestants and Orthodox, atheists, apostates and members of a minority religion, are not subjected to any limitation of the civil and political rights enjoyed by all citizens in the choices their consciences make.[2]

The principle that the state has no competence in religious questions is more complex, but its constituent elements are clear. There is a remarkable convergence of Christian thought and liberal thought on this notion: for different reasons, both affirm that it is not the task of the state to legislate on matters of dogmas, rites and religious doctrines. This assertion might seem to be contradicted by the existence, in some European countries, of state churches where the sovereign – who is also the head of the church – nominates the bishops and exercises functions relating to the government of religion. But these states – Denmark, England and Finland – seem less and less inclined to intervene in questions of faith and worship even when they have the possibility of doing so, and tend to reduce their own powers to a form of ratification of the decisions taken by ecclesiastical bodies. In 1993 Parliament approved the ordination of women to the priesthood which had been decided on by the General Synod of the Church of England; it would have been very difficult for Parliament to have introduced such a reform on its own initiative. In Western Europe the autonomy of the churches on matters of doctrine and organization was reinforced throughout the twentieth century, along with the consolidation of the notion of the secularity of the state, which had already been affirmed since the second half of the nineteenth century.

The third and last element which distinguishes relations between states and religious is their co-operation. Throughout Europe, after the collapse of the Communist regimes, co-operation between states and religions is the rule: it manifests itself in direct financing (as in Belgium, where the state pays the salaries of religious ministers) and in tax concessions; in a readiness to have chaplains in hospitals, prisons and the armed forces; in the teaching of religion in state schools; in free access of the religious confessions to the public mass media, and so on. Even secular and separatist France is no exception here: the military chaplains are paid by the state, and the maintenance of many Catholic churches is paid for with public funds. But everywhere in Europe this co-operation is selective. States do not collaborate in the same way with all religious communities: some receive more and others less, and yet others nothing at all. The readiness of states to collaborate with religious groups is greater where there is harmony between the values which regulate religious society and those which lie at the basis of civil society; it is less where this harmony does not exist. That is the reason why almost everywhere in Europe it is more complicated and expensive to build a mosque than to build a church, and explains why, in many countries, the Christian congregation of Jehovah's Witnesses proportionately pays more taxes than the Catholic Church: the concessions and contributions by the state are mainly directed towards those religious communities which, by virtue of the number of their members, the time they have been in a country or the political weight that they carry, are better integrated into the cultural and social traditions of a people and are in harmony with the rule and values that inspire it.

This model of relations between states and religions – characterized by freedom and religious equality at an individual level, by the autonomy of religious organizations and by selective collaboration between states and religions – has been the one adopted both by the countries which during the 1960s and 1970s emerged from Catholic confessionalism (Portugal, Spain and Italy), and those which more recently have abandoned or reformed the state church system (Sweden, Finland). Its basic features can be found in the legal ordering of many other countries of Western Europe (from Germany to Belgium, the Netherlands and France) and has provided the point of reference followed, though with persistent delays and resistance, by many ex-Communist countries which have recently entered the European Union. For these reasons the European system of relations between states and religions has appeared solid; its only weak point seemed to be an excessive inequality between the religious confessions, in particular in the countries of Central and Eastern Europe: if they succeeded in correcting this defect (as was vigorously requested by the United States after 1989), there was every indication that the system would be long-term. But things have proved to be more complicated than had been foreseen.

III. A model in process of transformation

The system of relationships between states and religions which I described in the previous section now seems to be being subjected to growing tensions which threaten to unbalance its equilibrium.

Over the last twenty years Europe has been involved in enormous transformations: the fading of Marxist ideology and the collapse of the Communist regimes; the growth of immigration and the emphasis on multi-culturalism in many countries of Western Europe; the weakening of the welfare state and economic systems based on the stability of the work-force; the decline of established styles of life and cultural models under the impact of globalization are only some of these changes.

The signs of this transformation are not unequivocal, and cannot remotely be put in a coherent framework; however, there is no doubt that they have brought a sense of disorientation and uncertainty to a large part of the European population, followed by a marked demand for identity, by a quest for symbols by which people can recognize themselves, and by a need for traditions which are shared and which will lead to sharing.[3] In this context religion has appeared to many people to be an important reservoir of values which can help them to respond to this demand. In the case of Christianity this religious revival has expressed itself in two ways. First, for a very narrow élite, this has constituted an intense experience of being born again, often experienced within church movements and communities which call for the total allegiance of their followers, in private and in public.

However, for the majority of Europeans, Christianity has not in fact proved to be a point of reference for choices about the family, leisure time, political activity or sexual life; sociological surveys confirm that the process of the secularization of private life is proceeding apace and not slowing down in any significant way. Yet these same surveys register a growing appreciation of the value of Christianity for culture and identity; many Europeans show a significant attachment to Christian religious symbols even when they observe few, if any, of the precepts of this religion and do not consider themselves members of any church. In Germany and Italy, for example, the battle to keep the crucifix in school halls has been waged by emphasizing the significance of the symbol in Western history and culture rather than its testimony to a specific religion: the value of the symbol for culture and identity counts more than its significance for faith. This makes it possible to gain support for the defence of a Christian symbol which is numerically greater than the sum total of those who believe or practise Christianity.

In Western Europe today (talk about the other European countries would have to be partially different), the secularization of private choices is no longer keeping step with the secularization of public institutions: it is going on without slowing down, whereas public secularization is showing signs of stopping. The split between the secularization of private life and the laicization of public life which has marked the greater part of the last two centuries seems to be a characteristic of post-modernity. Is this process of the reconversion of Christianity in the 'civil religion' of Europe destined to have an impact on the model of relationships between states and religions current in Europe?

IV. The juridical scenario of the future: a 'hypothesis'[4]

Why is this process still in its infancy? Why do the legal systems need time to receive and respect cultural and social transformations? This question is not easy to answer. However, it is probable that in the next few years there will be an increased tendency to distinguish between the traditional religions[5] – those which express the historical and cultural identity of a country – and all the others: Islam, new religious movements, religious minorities (one thinks, for example, of Catholicism in Russia). The distance between the former and the latter at the level of symbolic recognition and legal status will tend to increase. Probably that will have no direct consequences on the freedom and religious equality of individuals (in other words on the first characteristic of the model outlined at the beginning of this article), which are effectively protected by international law and by the constitutions of many countries; however, the autonomy of the religious confessions and above all collaboration between them and the state could become increasingly differentiated at the social, cultural and political roots which each religious group will be able to claim within a country.

In fact, in the eyes of states, the traditional religions – even though their following of convinced and practising believers is now small – have great importance in terms of social resources: they have a cultural profile (where the support of religion serves to give a solid foundation or European identity in the face of or against another civilization), an ethical profile (where recourse to religion is used to control a technological progress which is in process of abolishing all limits), and a political profile (where the religions are useful for reinforcing a stability and social cohesion which is put to hard tests by the process of immigration and terrorism). As a matter of principle this renewed attention to the social, cultural and political dimension includes all the religions: in reality, in particular the Christian religion and the Christian churches benefit from it, since they are the only ones which can claim a central role in the definition of European identity and can therefore present themselves as guardians of the 'memory' of Europe.

As for the function that the social resources of the Christian churches can still perform, the strategy of the liberalization of the European religious market supported by the United States is not viable. On the contrary, what is viable is some form of protectionism, of the kind that is expressed in the individualization of a group of religions and churches which are legally defined as 'traditional'. The laboratory of church politics which is now constituted by the ex-Communist countries of Europe is already experimenting with this solution, giving preference explicitly to the religions with a majority rooted in a country: in terms of registration, the acquisition of legal personhood, financing and so on. Moreover this system - in a rather more concealed way – is already in force in some countries of Western Europe.

V. The debate on the European Constitution[6]

It is within this context that the recent debate on the place of religion in the future European Constitution is to be placed and interpreted. At first sight this would seem a futile debate, centred on the opportunity to make a reference to Christianity in the constitutional Charter, i.e. in that part which the jurists consider to be of lesser importance. However, in reality the value of a constitution is not only legal but also political and cultural, and from this perspective the mention of Christianity is not in fact irrelevant.

The draft of the Constitution submitted for the approval of member states of the Union mentions religion at many points. It safeguards freedom and respects religious diversity, finding against any discrimination based on religions (Art.II-10, II-21, II-22 and III-8); it confirms that the idea of the religious freedom and equality of the individual is a platform shared by the majority of Europeans. Article 15 ensures that the status which the religious communities (and philosophical and non-confessional organizations) enjoy in the legal order of each national state will be respected and pledges the Union to maintain an 'open, transparent and regular' dialogue with them in such a way that autonomy and collaboration – i.e. the other two features of the European model of relations between states and religions – find a place in the future constitution of the Union. Where this could introduce a significant innovation with respect to the majority of the European national constitutions is in the preamble: apart from Greece, Ireland and Poland, none of the constitutions of the twenty-five member states of the Union refers to a specific religion in its preamble.[7] Then why do the Christian churches – and in particular the Catholic Church – insist so strongly on mentioning the Christian roots of Europe in the future European constitution?

The answer must be sought in the light of the attempt, which has already been mentioned, to transform Christianity into a great civil religion of Europe, emphasizing its character as custodian of the European memory and traditions. In this perspective it does not matter that the churches are increasingly empty; provided that the great Christian religions are capable of repositioning themselves on the ground of the European cultural heritage, they can become even more minorities yet at the same time continue to enjoy a relevant public role as the depositories of the European identity, providing symbols accepted by the whole of Europe. Here is the deep significance of the request to insert a reference to Christianity into the future constitution of the European Union. The recognition of the role played by Christianity in the formation of Europe is a guarantee of security. If the future is uncertain, the past can no longer be put in question and provides a solid foundation for the request that the Christian churches should continue to have a special position within the legal ordering of the Union; they merit the support of the public authorities not only because they bring about the support of the majority of European citizens (though in future that may no longer be the case), but also because they constitute a fundamental part of the tradition and identity of Europe. There are two difficult points along this road. The first consists in achieving a sufficient level of unity among the Christian churches, overcoming for example the conflicts which have seriously damaged the relations between the Catholic Church and some Orthodox churches; the second is the capacity to keep open the dialogue with a culture of lay and secular inspiration, rejecting intransigent obstinacy and sweeping condemnations. Unless Christianity can pass these two tricky crossroads in succession, it is improbable that it can present itself as the civil religion of all Europeans.

However, quite apart from these difficulties there remains the question of the appropriateness of mentioning Christianity – and only Christianity – in a text which has legal and political aims. In the historical and cultural sphere there is no doubt that of all the religions Christianity has played a unique role in the formation of Europe. But a constitution has to be an inclusive text, aimed at making the greatest possible number of citizens feel at home, so that it is impossible to forget the role – comparatively minor but by no means negligible – that Judaism has had in European history or that Islam seems destined to acquire, above all if Turkey becomes part of the Union. In 1997 the Catholic Church rightly protested because the Russian law on religious freedom omitted any reference to Catholicism in its preamble:[8] is it not a contradiction to call for a reference to Christianity in the European Constitution without mentioning the other religious entities which are no more minorities in Europe than Catholicism is in Russia?

For this reason it seems to me that there are only two possible choices. The first is to recall in the preamble of the future European Constitution at least the three great monotheistic religions which to different degrees have contributed to the formation of Europe. The second is to assert that Europe has religions which are not only humanistic but also religious. The first formula has greater evocative force; the second is weaker but also more inclusive. However, both prevent a reference limited to Christianity being read as the closedness of Europe to other religions and indicate that the different religious faiths play a complementary and not conflictual role in the construction of the united Europe.

Translated by John Bowden

Notes

1. I have developed the observations in this paragraph at greater length in 'The Legal Dimension' in Brigitte Maréchal, Stefano Allievi, Felice Dassetto and Jørgen Nielsen (eds), *Muslims in the Enlarged Europe. Religion and Society*, Leiden and Boston, MA 2003, pp. 219–54.
2. This last statement is not completely true of the countries, e.g. England, Denmark and Norway, where some state authorities are held to profess a particular religion; however, these are norms which, simply because they have a very great symbolic significance, interest a quite limited number of people.
3. For the observation which follows see the writings of Grace Davie (*Religion in Modern Europe. A Memory Mutates*, Oxford 2000; *Europe: The Exceptional Case. Parameters of Faith in the Modern World*, London 2002) and Danièle Hervieu-Léger ('Les tendances du religieux en Europe' in *Commissariat Général du Plan, Croyances religieuses, morales et éthiques dans le processus de construction européenne*, Paris 2002).
4. For a restatement at greater depth of the observations made in this paragraph see Silvio Ferrari, 'Religione, società e diritto in Europa occidentale', forthcoming in *Sociologia del diritto*, 2004/1.

5. Traditional religion must be redefined country by country: Catholicism is a traditional religion in Italy but not in Russia. Some religions – in particular the so-called new religious movements and Islam (with the exception of some regions of the Balkans and Russia) – are not traditional religions in any part of Europe. The case is different with Judaism, which is a minority religon but has contributed towards shaping the identity of Europe through Christianity.
6. On this debate see J. H. H. Weiler, *Un'europa cristiana. Un saggio esplorativo*, Milan 2003; Giovanni Reale, *Radici culturali e spirituali dell'Europa. Per una rinascita dell'uomo europo*, Milan 2003.
7. The Slovakian constitution refers to the 'spiritual heritage of Cyril and Methodius'; the German constitution refers to God.
8. Letter of John Paul II to President Yeltsin of Russia, 24 June 1997 (in *Il Regno-attualità*, 16/1997, pp. 464–5).

II. Europe, Christianity and Religions

Judaism and Europe: History and Counter-History

MICHAEL BRENNER

I. Europe and Jews

For two thousand years Europe has shaped Jewish history. The Jews, too, have contributed to this process. The role that the Jews have played in various areas cannot be demonstrated by statistics alone. All in all they have always been a small minority, but in societies usually dominated by Christians though sometimes also by Muslims they have fulfilled clearly defined theological and economic tasks. As the only non-Christian minority they were always particularly clearly perceived in Christianity, forced to the periphery of society, sometimes persecuted and expelled, but never completely hounded out of Europe.

We do not know where the earliest Jewish settlements in Europe were; however, the first evidence comes from Italy in the second century BCE. It may be significant for the later course of Jewish history that the first document which has come down to us speaks of an expulsion of the Jews. In 139 BCE they had to leave Rome, probably because they were seeking to gain proselytes, adherents to their religion. There were also Jewish settlements in other regions of Europe long before Christianity came to be known there. However, it was to be many centuries before Europe became a centre of Jewish life. Only after the completion of the Babylonian Talmud and after the downfall of the great academies in Mesopotamia was the European Diaspora given its firm place on the Jewish map.

1. An example of internationalism: the Talmud

Let's keep with the Talmud for a moment. No other document reflects the international character of Jewish culture more aptly than a page of the Babylonian Talmud. In the middle is the Mishnah, which came into being in Palestine during the first two centuries CE. To this are attached the discussions of the rabbis from the following three centuries which were written down in Babylon. The whole is surrounded by numerous layers in the margin, like the skins of an onion. Here we find the commentaries of Rashi from Troyes in France during the eleventh century alongside the Spanish scholars of the twelfth century, followed by Italian rabbis of the Renaissance and Polish scholars learned in the law from the sixteenth century. Reading this, the most important literary source for Judaism after the Hebrew Bible, reflects as it were in miniature the Jewish intellectual history of Europe over a millennium. Between Andalusia and Champagne, between Provence and Galicia, an alternative map of Europe was drawn which for centuries was important for a Jewish minority dispersed all over the continent and whose spiritual representatives often engaged in fruitful dialogue with their Christian and Muslim neighbours.

II. Persecution and creativity in the Jewish history of Europe

We can already see that to reduce the Jewish history of Europe to the poisoning of wells, legends of ritual murder, false accusations of desecrating the eucharistic host, crusades, Inquisition and ghetto would be as false as an idealization of European Jews as Minnesingers, rich merchants and senior court officials. Their history moved between the two poles of persecution and creativity, and often everyday experience with all its contradictions formed the centre of that history: the experience of people who felt at home in Worms, Toledo, Leghorn, Amsterdam, Saloniki and Lemberg and yet hoped for redemption in the Holy Land; who conversed in the language of their environment and prayed in Hebrew; who worked with their Christian neighbours but could not share in a meal with them. For centuries proximity and distance shaped the relationship of the Jews to their environment.

More than any other group, even in the pre-modern period Jews were Europeans, not least because of their mobility, their family ties and their activities as mediators between the cultures. It may be more than coincidence that from the mission which Charlemagne sent to the caliph Haroun al-Rashid, only the Jewish merchant Isaac from Narbonne returned and presented the emperor with an elephant as a gift from the caliph. Or we might think of the achievements of the Spanish Jews in mediating between ancient philosophy, Muslim culture and Christian civilization. Jews did not just act between the different parts of Europe, nor were they occupied only with intellectual transfers. It was by no means unusual for a Jewish man from Alsace to marry a Jewish woman from Württemberg or for a Polish scholar to work in Italy as a rabbi. And was there a more European family in the nineteenth century than the Rothschilds? Jews were also mediators in modernity, translators and bridge-builders between the nations. What would modern Europe be without Sigmund Freud, Albert Einstein, Franz Kafka or Arnold Schoenberg? And did not the anonymous Jews stamp the identity of Europe just as much as their Christian neighbours?

They were all to meet in Auschwitz: the Jews from the shtetel in Galicia, the port workers of Saloniki, the textile workers from Lodz, the cowherds from Franconia, the sophisticated city-dwellers from Berlin. A large part of Europe gathered here in the face of death. In Auschwitz, Europe was to bid farewell to its Jewish history.

III. Is a Jewish future in Europe possible?

Was it still possible to imagine a Jewish future in Europe after the catastrophe? After the devastating storm of the twentieth century the Jewish map of Europe also seemed to have taken on a quite different form; in collective Jewish memory Europe had been associated with notorious places and events. Immediately after the end of the war Samuel Gringauz, the spokesman for the liberated Jews in the American zone of occupied Germany, stated unmistakably what Europe meant to the few survivors: not Westminster Abbey or Versailles, not Strasbourg cathedral or the art treasures of Florence, but the mediaeval crusades, the Spanish Inquisition, the pogroms in Russia and the gas chambers of Auschwitz. He clearly called on the Jewish survivors to turn their backs on the whole continent. 'Farewell Europe!' was his motto.

Can there today, sixty years later, again be a Jewish future for Europe, a European future for Judaism? Views on this question differ widely. A few years ago the title given to the German edition of the provocative study by the distinguished British historian Bernard Wasserstein predicting the end of European Judaism was 'Europe without Jews'.[1] In England over the last three decades the Jewish community has lost a quarter of its members, and in some smaller countries it has declined by as much as a half. The reason for this democratic development is not antisemitism but assimilation. Every year, clearly fewer Jewish children are born than Jewish dead are buried.

Germany, the country in which the annihilation of European Jewry was planned, today represents the only Jewish community in Europe with a rapidly growing population. At the beginning of the twenty-first century German-Jewish society – leaving aside those states which took the place of the former Soviet Union – represented the third largest Jewish community in Europe, surpassed only by France and Great Britain. But even here the great sources of emigration from the countries which once formed the Soviet Union will soon dry up.

1. *An optimistic vision*

In an equally bold theory which points in precisely the opposite direction, the French political theorist Diana Pinto has developed an optimistic view of European Judaism. Against the background of the growing unification of Europe and increasing interest in its Jewish heritage she sees the possibility of the education of European Jews as a third pillar of Jewish society alongside Israel and American Jewry. In this vision the foundation of Jewish museums, academic institutions and cultural events, mostly by non-Jews, has also had its effect on a cultural renewal of Jewish life. Pinto detects a new curiosity about their own traditions among Jews, particularly among the new generation, of which they are often ignorant.[2]

If Europe is to grow together today, then European Jews will play a quite special role in this process. More than any other grouping, for centuries they were at home *all over* Europe and stamped by Europe; however, time and again in parts of this Europe they were persecuted, expelled and annihilated to an incomparably greater degree than any other group. What does Europe mean today for the Jews who have remained here? The spiritual centres of Troyes and Cordoba or the pogroms of Kischinev and the gas chambers of Auschwitz? Is their Europe that of Rashi and Maimonides, of Moses Mendelssohn, Sigmund Freud and Albert Einstein, or that of Torquemada, Chmielnicki and Hitler?

Like Samuel Gringauz, in the years after 1945 most Jews could not dream in their wildest imagination that Jewish life could once again flourish in the great cemetery which Europe has become for them. Today, after more than fifty years, however, other voices are being raised, as the theories of Bernard Wasserstein and Diana Pinto are making clear.

IV. The current discussion

The point in time for this discussion could hardly have been chosen more dramatically. Events between September 11 and the Iraq War may not have been able to produce a uniform identity, but they have created discontent among broad sectors of the Jewish population. There has never been a single Jewish voice and please God there will never be one as long as even two Jews are alive, but particularly over the last year a majority opinion has been forming among the Jews of Europe which stands in clear opposition to the majority opinion in the rest of Europe. There is no need always to be in agreement with the American government and the way in which it wages war. However, far less is there agreement with growing anti-Americanism: there may be dislike of the Sharon government, but there is even greater dislike of the anti-Israeli sentiments accumulating around it. Are Jews in Europe today felt to be trouble-makers, who want to corrupt the newly discovered delight in pacifism that exists in a peace-loving Europe? And is there not at least a tacit agreement that without Israel achieving peace in the Middle East would be child's play?

There can be no doubt that the basically optimistic mood prevailing ten years ago among the Jews of Europe has collapsed. The existence of the state of Israel may have been endangered in earlier times also, but today more and more Europeans seem to be indifferent or even hostile to the legitimacy of the Jewish state: Jewish institutions in Europe can no longer be recognized so much by the star of David or the Menorah as by the police cordon in front of them. A European study on antisemitism was suppressed for political reasons. All this does not mean that history is repeating itself. State antisemitism in Europe today is rightly taboo, and most Jews are well-integrated citizens of their nations and are certainly not exposed every day to the hideous face of antisemitism. Nevertheless a new uncertainty is growing.

Moreover this is nurtured by the fact that people do not know who their true friends are. Are they those who often have not yet come to terms with their Fascist past and understand the Arabs as an even greater threat than Israel, while at the same time calling on the Christian-Jewish West to keep the Muslims out of Europe? The Polish Jewish journalist Konstantyn Gebert found the answer to this: 'Whenever there is talk of a Christian-Jewish Europe I feel that I am a Muslim.' And what about those supposed friends who always claimed to be against the Fascists but now demonize America and complain that Israel is the real source of danger in the Middle East? The political dilemma of European Jews is complex, as is their relationship to the other non-Christian minority in Europe, which by now has grown far larger. On the one hand the European Muslims, as another minority, are natural allies, but on the other hand their radical ranks pose a real danger, as is evident above all in France. But even the relationship of European Jews to Israel itself is by no means simple. Every Jew knows that this state is not only a historical necessity but at the same time their last place of refuge – yet so many people find it difficult to identify with the policy of the present government.

V. Europe: unreservedly a state of many peoples?

Despite or precisely because of these numerous internal conflicts a gentle voice seems slowly to be gaining a hearing among one section of European Jewry, which seeks to communicate some messages to outsiders: it wants to communicate to a pluralistic Europe open to the world that there is a minority in its midst which has been at home on the continent for centuries; it wants to signal to American Jews that the scenario which is feared in some places of a new *Kristallnacht* in Paris or Berlin is unfounded hysteria; and finally it wants to make the liberal political camp in Israel understand that it also has conversation partners in Europe who have open ears. In a Europe in process of expansion the Jewish minority can build small but not unimportant bridges with America and the Middle East, and in a climate of political polarization it can represent a radical voice of moderation.

This voice must not be underestimated. We need only look at the past. In a Habsburg empire plagued by conflicts between nationalities the Jews were told that in the end they were the only ones who could identify unreservedly with this state of many peoples; the others were Germans or Czechs or Hungarians first and foremost. Should the experiment of European union succeed despite all the prophecies of doom, perhaps the other Europeans could perhaps even discover how much of European cultural history is to be found on one page of the Talmud.

Translated by John Bowden

Notes

1. Bernard Wasserstein, *Vanishing Diaspora: The Jews in Europe since 1945*, Cambridge, MA 1996.
2. See e.g. Diana Pinto, A *New Jewish Identity for Post-1989 Europe*, Policy Paper no.1, June 1996, Institute for Jewish Policy Research, London, and ead., 'Europa – ein neuer "jüdischer Ort"', *Menora* 10, 1999, pp. 15–34.

The Ecumenical Movement in Europe: Challenges and Conflicts

REINHARD FRIELING

European politicians often make assessments of the contribution of the churches to the process of European union and meaningfully add as an expectation for the future: 'We need their voice; not, however, separately but as a trinity of the Catholic, Orthodox and Protestant traditions.'

On the basis of the principle 'Unity is Strength', the view of the politicians is not only understandable but certainly worth taking to heart by the churches. A shared view expressed by the churches carries more weight with political authorities than a diversity of church positions which politicians are not really able to evaluate and put in context. However, a shared view presupposes that the churches have arrived at a consensus on certain substantive questions and that they are in a position to formulate this consensus together and to present it jointly to the political authorities.

I. Basic consensus

Numerous ecumenical studies and declarations – not least the two European Ecumenical Assemblies in Basle in 1989 and Graz in 1997 – attest that there is a fundamental Christian consensus on most socially relevant questions.[1] In its Chapter 3 (nos 7–12) the *Charta Oecumenica*,[2] too, describes numerous shared Christian principles on the basis of which the churches want to play a part in shaping Europe, so this could really meet the expectations of politicians.

Since the Second Vatican Council the theological dialogues between the churches have produced a surprisingly large number of convergence and consensus texts in which at least the ecumenical commissions present a broad basic consensus on central matters of faith. 'What we share is more important than what still divides us' is said time and again. Therefore despite the confessional clashes which still persist, much ecumenical fellowship is possible, not only on questions of practical and above all social collaboration but also in so-called spiritual ecumenism, in praying and worshipping together.

Alongside this there is the experience that at the various levels of church life the fronts of serious disputes among theologians and laity on world views and faith often run right across the confessions and that the 'conservatives' and 'progressives' of any church seem closer to one another than the other group in one's own confession.

At the European level there are two organizations which speak and act for the official church institutions and which work relatively well together at an executive level. The Conference of European Churches (CEC) as an ecumenical gathering comprises almost all non-Roman Catholic churches (Orthodox, Anglicans, Old Catholics, Lutherans, Reformed, Methodists, Baptists and other Protestant free churches); it has offices in Geneva, Brussels and Strasbourg. The Council of the Roman Catholic Episcopal Conferences in Europe (CCEE) has its base in St Gallen (in Brussels there is also the Commission of Catholic Episcopal Conferences, COMECE, drawn from the member states of the European Union and the Apostolic nuncio to the European institutions). A joint committee of these two bodies considers regularly whether and how a common standpoint of the churches on questions relevant to Europe is possible.

A good deal of church involvement takes place at a European level through the network of church organizations and associations for peace and justice. Welfare work and charitable activities, education, migration, women, men, young people, etc. Some of these organizations work together in an ecumenical alliance, sometimes even as integrated organizations.

II. The confessions remain

On the other hand, in all soberness it must be noted that the churches are only 'on the way towards visible communion of the churches in Europe' (thus the title of the second chapter of the *Charta Oecumenica*) and that the capacity to speak as churches with one voice still has to be developed. The reality of parallel and partially competing confessional identities time and again makes individual churches go their own ways. The hope that the various Christian traditions would resolve on a single institution is as realistic as the prospect that all the European states would sweepingly renounce their state sovereignty in favour of a European union.

Alongside the confessional differences a further plurality in the position of the churches in Europe is significant, namely the marked cultural and national stamp of individual churches. For centuries the scene has been not so much the one Europe as a division into the East moulded by Byzantium (with the Orthodox churches) and a western West (with the Roman Catholic Church and the churches that grew out of the Reformation). Various philosophies and legal systems have stamped the cultures and also the churches with their theologies; here and there this is felt sometimes as a distancing alienation and sometimes as a mutual enrichment. In the West there is, roughly speaking, the so-called 'two swords theory' and a variety of relationships between the church and state, with notions of a 'Christian society' and – above all after the Enlightenment – various attitudes to the secular state and to 'laicism'. The Byzantine East has always praised the model of symphony, with a tendency to identify the community of believers with the nation and the state as the external guardian of faith and the church. The martyrdoms experienced under Communist rule have still not banished the tendency, for example in Russia, to emphasize the concept of Orthodox nations and to regard this positively as a value pointing towards the future rather than conservatively as a survival of past centuries.

All the confessional churches emphasize that the church is by nature universal and that its fellowship is not grounded in any national, cultural or linguistic community, but rather in faith in Christ and in baptism. However, all over Europe there has been a close connection between the church and national cultures. Here the churches have been a 'cultural factor' in that for example they helped to shape 'Catholic Poland', 'Orthodox Russia' or 'Lutheran Scandinavia'. Even the widespread secularization of public life and the exodus from the churches in most European countries has not done away with this cultural stamp. At the same time the churches were and are a 'product of culture' in that for example French Catholicism, Greek Orthodoxy and German Protestantism are to this day moulded by specific spiritualities and mentalities.

Over recent centuries the dovetailing of church and culture have led the churches to reflect in a new and self-critical way on the relationship between homeland, nation, people, state and church. The various church structures which have come into being through history have so far remained very stable, as witness the Orthodox 'national churches' in the East, the various 'state churches' and 'folk churches' in the West, and the diversity of most small 'free churches'. Around 90% of all European churches are either large majority churches or small minority churches in their countries. Only in central Europe, above all in Germany, is there a confessional mixture of around 50% Catholics and 50% Protestants. Such differing presuppositions of course have major consequences for the ecumenical experiences and attitudes of Christians and churches. The ecumenical standpoint is very difficult in the churches and countries of Europe.

With the 'Guidelines for the Growing Collaboration between the Churches in Europe' laid down in the *Charta Oecumenica* in 2001 the two representative assemblies of the churches in Europe have entered into twenty-six ecumenical 'commitments', which the individual churches and episcopal conferences are to adopt and sign. The *Charta Oecumenica* has been translated into thirty languages and in some countries (e.g. the Netherlands, Hungary and Germany) has already been signed in solemn ceremonies within the framework of the national councils of churches by senior representatives of the church.

However, neither the CCEE or the CEC assume responsibility for the teaching authority of the churches involved, so that the introduction to the *Charta Oecumenica* reads: 'However, it has no magisterial or dogmatic character, nor is it legally binding under church law. Its authority will derive from the voluntary commitments of the European churches and ecumenical organizations.'

So the *Charta* did not bring any breakthrough in the direction of the resolution of the dogmatic controversies between the churches, but it is a new start towards a greater ecumenical fellowship among the European churches. At any rate the *Charta Oecumenica* is the first joint ecumenical document from the European churches for a millennium. In it the signatory churches enter into serious commitments which to date are far from being met by the ecumenical status quo.

III. The confessional problem

The situation that I have described logically leads to the question of what the dogmatic obstacles to a union of the churches are, even though a consensus has been arrived at in the fundamentals of belief in the triune God.

The answer is that the confessions draw different conclusions from the basic consensus over the question how the gospel is communicated and what role the church, the sacraments and the ministry have in it. To put it more formally: the confessions are essentially one in belief in the triune God but differ over what they believe about themselves, about the church and its authority, and about the authorities in the church.

The question whether these differences must really divide the church or whether they can be an expression of a legitimate diversity within the one church of Christ is vigorously disputed and lies at the very heart of the confessional problem itself. The point at issue is how the relationship of particular confessional churches to the one church of Jesus Christ is regarded. Is there an identity which makes only one's own church fully the church and justifies the claim that others are not churches in the true sense? Or is the unity of the church given in faith in Christ, manifesting itself in the fellowship and reciprocal recognition of the confessional churches which have grown up in history with different church structures?

With the words of the Niceno-Constantinopolitan creed of 381 the *Charta Oecumenica* has stated: 'We believe in "the one, holy, catholic and apostolic church".' 'Our paramount ecumenical task is to show forth this unity, which is always a gift of God.' And it commits itself in the following words: 'We commit ourselves in the power of the Holy Spirit, to work towards the visible unity of the Church of Jesus Christ in the one faith, expressed in the mutual recognition of baptism and in eucharistic fellowship, as well as in common witness and service' (*Charta Oecumenica* 1).

1. Most Orthodox representatives assented to these formulations in the *Charta Oecumenica*. However, the Russian Orthodox Church claimed that they were notably deficient.[3] It argued that here, in a typically Protestant way, the ecumenical movement became interchangeable with the church of Christ. The unity of the church had never been lost and did not need to be restored visibly; it was already attested visibly with the decisions of the councils of the early church and was preserved in the Orthodox churches. A call for repentance and renewal had to be made to those who had fallen away from this unity of the church. It was ecclesiologically incorrect to speak of belonging to Christ in a way which transcended all the confessions. If we are separated, then we are separated in Christ. The attempt to divide doctrine into what is 'fundamental' and what is not and then to say that we are separated only by secondary questions of doctrine was unacceptable to the Orthodox.

A series of other Orthodox theologians criticizes this Russian Orthodox position as one-sided and too radical, because insufficient value is attached to the Christian faith of those who are not Orthodox. But the view from Moscow makes it clear that an ecclesiological consensus is still remote.

2. At almost the same time as the statement by the Moscow Synod of Bishops in 2000, the Roman Catholic Congregation for the Doctrine of Faith published the declaration *Dominus Iesus. On the Unicity and Salvific Universality of Jesus Christ and the Church*.[4] This states that the one church of Christ which we confess in the creed 'subsists' only in the Roman Catholic Church, whereas the other churches and ecclesial communities have only

'elements of sanctification and truth' which are 'forces impelling towards Catholic unity'.[5] The Orthodox are said to lack full communion with the Catholic Church because they do not accept the Roman Catholic doctrine of the primacy of the pope. And of the Reformation churches it is said: 'The ecclesial communities which have not preserved the valid episcopate and the genuine and integral substance of the eucharistic mystery, are not churches in the proper sense' (no.17).

This Roman Catholic ecclesiological self-awareness does not exclude the closest possible collaboration with other churches and ecclesial communities when it is a matter of shared beliefs and ethical positions.[6] But it is clear that in the Roman Catholic understanding, authentically only the pope and his curia and below them the Roman Catholic bishops are responsible for the magisterial and public statements of the church of Christ and that ecumenical collaboration must not infringe this authority.

The post-synod brief of Pope John Paul II *Ecclesia in Europa* dated 28 June 2003 makes clear what terminology and what conception of ecumenical relations follow from the eccclesiological principles. The 'church in Europe' is spoken of in the singular and primarily the Roman Catholic Church is envisaged. The need for ecumenical collaboration is mentioned only in connection with further challenges; the *Charta Oecumenica*, for which (only) the Council of European Episcopal Conferences was responsible, is not mentioned here.

Certainly many Roman Catholic ecumenists, too, are disappointed at this Roman style and Roman centralism. All in all, however, it is clear why it is so difficult for the churches to speak with one voice.

3. The Protestant churches likewise display an ecclesiological sense that the one church of Jesus Christ is realized (*subsistit*) in them and that the true unity of the church is already given in Christ. However, that does not exclude the recognition of the church of Jesus Christ in other confessional churches, and according to a formulated consensus on the shared understanding of the gospel, full 'church fellowship in words and sacrament' can then follow, along with the obligation to shared witness and service in the world. However, there is no united organization nor a unitary institution with a joint church leadership.

This model is realized in the Leuenberg church fellowship of Lutheran, Reformed, United and Methodist churches in Europe. With its declaration 'The Church of Jesus Christ. The Reformation Contribution to the Ecumenical Dialogue on Church Unity', for the first time since the Reformation the Vienna Assembly of 1994 presented something like a joint Protestant church constitution.⁷ Moreover there are bilateral statements of reciprocal recognition and church fellowship, e.g. the Meissen Declaration between the Church of England and the Evangelical Church in Germany of 1988 and the Porvoo Declaration between the Anglican Churches in Great Britain and the Lutheran Church in Scandinavia and the Baltic.

There is still no official 'church fellowship' between other Protestant churches, but there is a reciprocal invitation to the eucharist. In the Conference of European Churches and in the national ecumenical councils (the Working Parties of the Christian Churches) some Protestant free churches, Pentecostal churches and new charismatic confessions have taken their place alongside the larger traditional churches; these are often organized only on a national and not yet on a European level.

The diversity of confessionally conditioned ecclesiological and organizational options certainly makes it difficult for Protestants in Europe to speak with one voice. Indeed, many churches do not even want this and prefer to live in their own self-satisfied way. For many Protestant churches and Christians an official acceptance of the *Charta Oecumenica* would be an enormous ecumenical step forward.⁸

It is an extremely important task in the contribution of the churches to the process of European union for them to clarify ecclesiologically and practically the mandate of the trans-national and inter-confessional ecumenical organizations in Europe. For example, does each church present its own interests to the European Union? Or are the churches ready to give the Conference of European Churches a mandate to speak and act for them there?

The principle of the universal church which in one way or another all churches acknowledge should lead to the creation at all geographical levels of those shared ecumenical structures which make the proclamation of the gospel most effective in word and deed. However, among the majority of Orthodox and Protestant churches the 'autonomy', the 'autocephaly', or the 'sovereignty' of their own national, state or free church plays such a major role that the trans-confessional and trans-national ecumenical bodies are regarded only as service organizations for safeguarding their own interests (not by ecumenists, but by many officials and also church people). The statement by one Protestant church leader after an ecumenical service of worship is symptomatic: 'Ecumenism is all very well, but it's far better if we're on our own.'

Granted, the Roman Catholic Church has in the Vatican an effective body for speaking and acting at a European level, but a readiness for joint actions with other churches comes up against its limits when its own authority might be infringed, as is manifested, say, in the diplomatic activity of the apostolic nunciatures and in the statements and actions of the pope and his curia.

IV. Contributing to the shape of Europe

The *Charta Oecumenica* for the growing collaboration of the churches in Europe goes beyond the confessional and ecumenical status quo depicted here in that independently of confessionally conditioned ecclesiological principles and some problems of institutions and functionaries, in the third chapter it describes some principles for 'Our Common Responsibility in Europe'.

Instead of dreaming in a utopian or conservative fashion of a 'Christian Europe', the Charta soberly begins from a Europe 'between the Atlantic and the Urals, between the North Cape and the Mediterranean' which has a pluralistic religious and world-view. However, this is no cause for false modesty, but on the contrary emphasizes a challenge: 'The most important task of the churches in Europe is the common proclamation of the Gospel, in both word and deed, for the salvation of all' (no.2). 'With the Gospel, we want to stand up for the dignity of the human person created in God's image and, as churches together, contribute towards reconciling peoples and cultures' (Introduction). It is recalled that 'through the centuries Europe has developed a primarily Christian character in religious and cultural terms'. And it is emphasized that 'our Christian faith and love for our neighbours is a source of hope for morality and ethics, for education and culture, and for political and economic life, in Europe and throughout the world' (no.7).

These words emphasize above all the responsibility of each individual Christian to contribute towards shaping Europe in the light of the Christian faith. The task of the churches as international communities in Europe is described like this:

> The churches support an integration of the European continent. Without common values, unity cannot endure. We are convinced that the spiritual heritage of Christianity constitutes an empowering source of inspiration and enrichment for Europe. On the basis of our Christian faith, we work towards a humane, socially conscious Europe, in which human rights and the basic values of peace, justice, freedom, tolerance, participation and solidarity prevail. We likewise insist on the reverence for life, the value of marriage and the family, the preferential option for the poor, the readiness to forgive, and in all things compassion (no.7).

Here the concerns of the ecumenical conciliar process for justice, peace and the integrity of creation are taken up and related to Europe; however, it is clearly emphasized that 'any Eurocentrism is to be avoided' and 'the responsibility of Europe for the whole of humankind is to be reinforced'.

Some of the details of these principles are not specifically Christian, but are also the concern of other religious and ideological groupings. So in its closing part the *Charta Oecumenica* goes into fellowship with Judaism, relations with Islam and the encounter with other religions and world-views and emphasizes the need for dialogue and a readiness 'to pursue with them matters of common concern' (no. 12). The term 'ecumenical' is not used for these relations. However, it is 'ecumenically' significant in terms of the inter-confessional and international relationships of the Christian churches that with the *Charta Oecumenica* the churches have arrived at common principles for relations with the other religions and for Christian mission and evangelization in Europe.

In addition to this, in view of the dominant role of the European Union, it is now urgently necessary for more justice to be done to the commitment expressed in no.7 of the *Charta Oecumenica*: 'We commit ourselves to seek agreement with one another on the substance and goals of our social responsibility, and to represent in concert, as far as possible, the concerns and visions of the churches *vis-à-vis* the secular European institutions.'

The ecumenists in the churches are largely already fulfilling these commitments, but the institutional churches as a whole still have a great deal of catching up to do ecumenically. When the new constitution of the European Union comes into force there should be a regular discussion between the responsible bodies and persons in the European Union and the churches. Here the churches have the opportunity, say in connection with questions of bioethics, the protection of life, migration, the fight against poverty, education and culture, etc., to present the church's position jointly and to help to shape Europe in a Christian spirit.

Translated by John Bowden

Notes

1. *Frieden in Gerechtigkeit* (The Official Documents of the European Ecumenical Assembly in Basle 1989), Basle and Zurich 1989; *Versöhnung. Gabe Gottes und Quelle neuen Lebens* (The Official Documents of the Second European Ecumenical Assembly in Graz 1997), Graz, Vienna and Cologne 1998.
2. *Charta Oecumenica. Leitlinien für die wachsende Zusammenarbeit unter den Kirchen in Europa*, produced by the (Roman Catholic) Conference of Bishops in Europe and the Conference of European Churches, St Gallen und Geneva 2001.

3. Letter from the Moscow Patriarchate to the Conference of European Churches dated 4 July 2000, in the CEC archive. The synod of bishops in Moscow expressed themselves in basically the same terms a little later, in August 2000, but with more qualifications: 'Grundlegende Prinzipien der Beziehung der Russischen Orthodoxen Kirche zu den Nicht-Orthodoxen', *Orthodoxie aktuell,* September 2000, pp. 6–12, and *ÖkumenischeRundschau* 50, 2001, pp. 210–15.
4. English text at www.cin.org/docs/dominus-iesus.html.
5. Vatican II Constitution on the Church, *Lumen gentium,* no.8.
6. Cf. the encyclical *Ut unum sint* of 25 May 1995 at www.cin.org/jp2ency/jp2utunu.html. and 'Directory for the Principles and Norms of Ecumenism' of 25 March 1993, at www.adoremus.org/EcumenismNorms.html.
7. Wilhelm Hüffmeier (ed), *Die Kirche Jesu Christi,* Leuenberger Texte 1, Frankfurt am Main 1995. This volume contains the English version, 'The Church of Jesus Christ. The Contribution of the Reformation towards Ecumenical Dialogue on Church Unity'.
8. E.g. *Charta Oecumenica,* no.3: 'We commit ourselves to overcome the feeling of self-sufficiency within each church, and to eliminate prejudices; to seek mutual encounters and to be available to help one another.' No. 4: 'We commit ourselves to act together at all levels of church life wherever conditions permit and there are no reasons of faith or overriding expediency militating against this.'

Euro-Islam: Challenge or Opportunity?

KARL-JOSEF KUSCHEL

Before we investigate the concept of Euro-Islam in the narrower sense, the topic needs to be put in a historical context.

I. European identity versus Judaism and Islam

Two intellectual and cultural traditions, Christianity and humanism, play a dominant role in the way in which Europe defines itself. Most Europeans would describe their history as the consequence of two thrusts towards pluralization: in the eleventh and sixteenth centuries the Christian unity of Europe which had existed hitherto was torn apart; there was a juxtaposition and opposition of confessions within Christianity – Orthodoxy, Catholicism and Protestantism. In the eighteenth century a second thrust towards pluralization made itself felt: the unity of Christianity in so far as it still existed was once again torn apart, and most European societies split into one part with ties to the Christian churches and one part with a secular humanistic orientation. The fact that for centuries there had been a living Judaism and a living Islam in Europe played hardly any role in the way in which many Europeans defined themselves as Europeans.

In the case of Judaism, we are talking of a negligible minority. Moreover, Judaism was regarded by a latent or open European anti-Judaism and anti-semitism as an alien body which had to be removed – through assimilation or annihilation. The practice of contempt for and discrimination against Europe and then its annihilation is also part of European, and especially German, history. So the European identity has always *also* had an anti-Jewish dimension.

Islam too has played above all a negative role in the history of European self-awareness and self-definition. There is a serious discussion among historians as to whether what is called 'European identity' did not first arise in the Middle Ages, when Europe began to defend itself against the 'threat from Islam'. We may not want to go as far as the Belgian historian Henri Pirenne, who has spoken of the 'birth of the West' from anti-Islamic feelings with the slogan 'Muhammad made Charlemagne possible',[1] but according to the most recent research of the Italian historian Franco Cardini, it is possible to speak of a common European consciousness only with the *reconquista* in Spain in connection with Santiago de Compostela.² So 'European identity' a priori has an anti-Islamic dimension

II. A past which is still alive: the baneful legacy of the *reconquista*

All this is evident when we have to reconstruct European history with respect to Judaism and Islam largely as a history of catastrophe. Instead of a story of guaranteed co-existence and acceptance for the most part we have a history of discrimination, rejection and indeed extermination. The history of European Jewry threatened to end with the mass exodus of Jews or their mass extermination in the Nazi concentration camps of Auschwitz, Treblinka and Maidanek. And what about the history of European Islam?

There was already a living Islam in two regions of Europe. One region was Sicily. The island was conquered in 902 and for around 150 years it was ruled solely by Muslims. Only in the eleventh century did the Normans under Robert Guiscard in collaboration with the pope (Nicholas II granted it on him as a fiefdom in 1059) succeed in subjecting the Muslims there. However, Norman Christian rulers like Roger I and Roger II practised tolerance towards the Muslim inhabitants, so that a unique *convivencia* became possible and Christian churches stood side by side with mosques in a juxtaposition of Western Christian and Arab Muslim civilizations. If we follow a German historian like Eberhard Horst, 'For a period Sicily served as a model. In no other country of mediaeval Christendom apart from Moorish Spain was there comparable co-existence in mutual toleration.'³

The man who was later to become the emperor Frederick II grew up in this multi-religious and multi-cultural context of Sicily. He took contact with Muslims for granted, spoke Arabic and got to know Arab thought and Arab culture. Granted, in Frederick's time the majority of Saracens had left Palermo and other larger places on the island and predominantly sought refuge in the mountains of western Sicily, but an Arab way of life was in the air that Frederick breathed. Palermo was regarded as a multilingual cultural centre in which Latin, Greek and Arab culture were interwoven. Moreover none of the Christian rulers of the Middle Ages was better prepared for a different basic attitude to Islam than Frederick II. That had its effect above all on his policy over crusades and in the fact that Frederick allowed between 16,000 and 20,000 Muslims to have their own settlement on the high plain of Lucera, just over ten miles north-west of Forggia in Southern Italy.

Frederick's opponents used this 'scandal' as a weapon against him, and even during his lifetime he found himself exposed to the charge of heresy, indeed blasphemy. After his death his enemies set to work. The Muslims of Lucera, now with no personal protection from the emperor, succumbed to brutal extermination. Charles II of Anjou, king of Naples, had Lucera destroyed in 1300; the Muslim inhabitants were massacred and the few survivors sold into slavery. All this was with the approval of the papal curia. The 'pagan colony' founded by Frederick was to be razed to the ground for all time, and the 'scandal' on Christian soil was to be effaced. The walls of Lucera were burnt down and dismantled. Now for centuries there was no shared life between Jews, Christians and Muslims in this part of the world.

History took a similar course in Spain around 200 years later. Since its conquest by the Muslims in 711 and the establishment of the caliphate of Cordoba, for centuries there had likewise been a *convivencia* between Jews, Christians and Muslims on the Iberian peninsula.[4] Cultural and religious coexistence had become possible – though it was ambivalent and is certainly not to be idealized. However, in the course of the crusader movements, in Spain too a mood of *reconquista* had arisen which reached a nadir in 1478 in the introduction of the Inquisition, now also organized by the state. Up to 9,000 *auto da fés*, executions usually by burning at the stake, must be set to the account of one of the most evil figures of church history, the Grand Inquisitor Thomas de Torquemada. Accepted as an ordinary state authority responsible for policing and justice, his Inquisition raged inexorably above all against Jews and Muslims who had only superficially converted to Christianity.

The final end of the *convivencia* came in 1492 with the 'Christian' conquest of the city of Granada. Jews were either brutally compelled to accept baptism (it is estimated that there were around 240,000 forced conversions) or were immediately expelled (around 170,000 of them). In the long run the same thing happened to the Muslims. In 1525 ordinances decreeing compulsory baptisms were issued, and these were applied even more mercilessly from 1567 on. A great Muslim rebellion a year later, which was put down with great bloodshed, was only the beginning of the final end of Islam in Spain. This came in 1609 with a decree by King Philip III and led to an expulsion and deportation of once again around 150,000 people, which was now carried out in a highly organized way.

III. Sarajevo – a house with four entrances

Bosnia-Herzegovina is the only region of Europe in which Jews, Christians and Muslims continued to live together for centuries. No region has such a multi-confessional and multi-religious complexity. To the three cultural groupings, Muslim Bosnian, Orthodox Serbian and Catholic Croat, from the sixteenth century (after the expulsion of the Jews from Spain) there was added a fourth – Sephardic Jewish. Moritz Levy, the Chief Rabbi of Sarajevo, described this impressively as early as 1911 in his book on 'The Sephardim in Bosnia'. The Bosnian Historian Kemal Barkarsic produced a new edition of the work in 1966 and pointed out: 'Levy's work is a unique well-founded testimony which has not been surpassed, a fundamental source of cultural history relating to the Jewish components of the distinctive features of Bosnia-Herzegovina, an open house with four entrances.'[5] Beyond question, this juxtaposition and co-existence of Jewish, Christian and Muslim cultures created that extraordinarily complex situation which historians of Bosnia-Herzegovina say led on the one hand to a 'cultural and intellectual isolationism' and on the other to 'becoming used to otherness as a normal part of life'.[6]

So for more than five hundred years Jews, Christians and Muslims lived together in this region. However, Western Europe largely ignored this fact. Only when war broke out in the 1990s did a shock wave run through Europe – born of the fear that other Europeans could become involved. Even Christians in the Balkans, although they too had suffered under the Communist oppression in Tito's Yugoslavia, evidently did not understand that in their region, on European soil, a historically unique model existed; otherwise perhaps they would have become involved earlier and more intensively in inter-confessional and inter-religious collaboration.

No one among the Christian churches of Europe did anything to remind Christians from Lisbon to Warsaw of this and make them aware that two historical models of the co-existence of Jews, Christians and Muslims in Europe had already failed in disastrous ways: with the annihilation of the Muslims in Sicily in the thirteenth century and the annihilation of Judaism and Islam in Spain from the fifteenth century on. So twice in its history Europe had the opportunity to learn constructive lessons from the co-existence of Jews, Christians and Muslims; twice this was a disastrous failure. Bosnia-Herzegovina and Kosovo are the third opportunity.

It is encouraging that European literature is sending out counter-signals. The most significant author in contemporary Spanish literature, Juan Goytisolo, is one of them. His 'Notes from Sarajevo' appeared in 1993, written on a stay there during the war. Goytisolo is one of the few writers who has preserved a sensitivity to the multi-religious dimension of European, and especially Spanish, culture. His work is one long plea to regard the co-existence of Jews, Christians and Muslims as an opportunity to enrich

Europe. He calls the expulsion of Muslims from Spain a self-mutilation on the part of European culture. In his Sarajevo book we can read: 'Many Europeans are still imprisoned in the patterns of a historical past of Christians and Muslims. The spectres of the past act as nightmares in their unconscious.'[7] Or even more sharply in his travel book into the world of Islam (2000): 'Islam is the other side, the negative side of Europe, the subject of its aversion and a constant temptation.'[8]

IV. The new religious situation in Europe

However, Europe can no longer ignore this multi-religious history of Bosnia-Herzegovina, since it is itself entangled in a historical process of the formation of multi-religious minorities. There are now once again 100,000 Jews and around 3 million Muslims in Germany.[9] In France there are 4 million Muslims, in Britain 3 million. Estimates predict that by 2020 there may possibly be 20 million Muslims in Europe. There have never been such strong religious minorities, for example in Germany. Even Jewry, which in the twentieth century was the largest religious and cultural minority, amounted to only around 600,000 people at the beginning of the 1930s. So there has never been a religious minority numbering millions in Germany, and this religion has never been Islam. Other European countries face similar developments. It follows from this that all European societies find themselves confronted with social and political challenges for which they are unprepared.

Neither most Europeans nor most Muslims have taken in this new situation in Europe. That is evident from the political debates over a European or national culture which keep flaring up, or the question whether Islamic countries like Turkey also belong in Europe. There are disputes among Muslims over how they should relate to modern, democratic Europe. Islamophobia, and indeed resentment, dominates debates in some places; anti-secularistic and anti-modern prejudices in others. For most Muslims, too, at present see themselves in a quite novel situation in Europe. For the first time a substantial number of them live outside the *Dar al-Islam* – in countries whose legislation is not based on the Shariah. They have an equally heated discussion about the future of Islam in Europe. Which model are they to go by? What are the options? Are European and Islamic values compatible?[10]

V. What is 'Euro-Islam'?

The concept of Euro-Islam was introduced into discussions about politics and political theory in Germany at the beginning of the 1990s by the Göttingen political theorist Basam Tibi. Since then it has been put forward time and again in numerous publications.[11] Here from the start 'Euro-Islam' means more than a description of the fact that Islam is also being practised more and more in Europe, and therefore means more than Islam *in* Europe. Granted, the concept is *also* a reaction to the fact that – in the course of the economic pressures and needs of Western European industrialized states since the 1960s – more and more people of the Muslim faith are living in Europe, above all in the major conurbations. 'Immigrant workers' are increasingly becoming citizens, the 'labour force' are becoming neighbours and immigrants are become native citizens. During the course of the 1980s these people also began to make themselves visible as believers – by building mosques, by establishing Islamic cultural centres, Islamic cemeteries, indeed a whole Islamic infrastructure. So 'Euro-Islam' is the consequence of the fact that a considerable number of Muslims no longer have to, indeed want to, live in a context stamped by Islam, but in one stamped by the West and by Christianity.

However, 'Euro-Islam' sets out to denote more than an empirically indisputable fact. The term sums up a spirit which strives to make Islam compatible with the spirit of Europe, or more precisely with the political values of European modernity. It does not want a simple 'Westernization' of Islam, nor does it want to claim the whole world for Islam. Rather, it is tailored to being a Muslim in the context of Europe. Programmatically it puts forward the counter-concept to an understanding of 'Islam in Europe', in which the Muslim as a member of the *Dar-al-Islam* is still subject to the Shariah. This in particular is the understanding of a conservative and reactionary Islamism, which in a totalitarian way maintains the fiction of a unitary Islam for Muslims all over the world and defines this uniformity by the Shariah. As such it also calls for recognition in Europe. 'Islam *in* Europe' therefore means the recognition of a traditional and unchanged Islam, exploiting the concept of multi-culturality which is already guaranteed by the constitution in most European countries. According to this concept Muslims have their own niche, as do all other religious, cultural or ethnic minorities. And they want to practise their Islam unchanged in this niche, as if moving from Ankara to Amsterdam, from Cairo to Copenhagen, from Fez to Frankfurt, was merely a change of scene.

However, for advocates of a 'Euro-Islam', that has produced a social paradox which in the long run must lead to intolerable tensions. Contrary to its intentions, the concept of multi-culturality in particular does not encourage integration but the cementing of parallel societies, indeed counter-societies, to existing secular societies. Muslims form an Umma, a community in solidarity, which, unheeding of the new culture, deliberately distinguishes itself from the non-Muslim environment by practising the Islamic religious law, indeed is concerned even to permeate the non-Muslim world with Islam and thus in the long term carry on a mission.

The concept of 'Euro-Islam' forms the decisive alternative to this concept of an 'Islam *in* Europe'. It uses the existence of Islam in Europe to change traditional Islam in the light of the legal and political values which have grown up in Europe. According to Tibi there are five normative foundations of European modernity which the legitimacy of any democratic commonwealth produces. A 'Euro-Islam' must respect these normative foundations if it is to be worthy of the name:

(a) *Pluralism* at every level, but in the institutionally and legally binding framework of the set of rules of a consensus which is obligated to modern culture. The recognition of such pluralism by Muslims entails that they do not understand themselves as separate but as an integral part of the pluralistic whole. This means no Islamic mission in Europe, thus doing away with visions of conquest and dualistic confrontational thought which encourage divisions in society: the house of Islam = the house of war. The distant goal of an 'Islamicization of Europe', which for tactical reasons is not always stated plainly, must be clearly renounced.

(b) *Tolerance* along the lines of the Enlightenment and modern culture. This means no longer just the 'toleration' of Christians and Jews as a 'protection which is commanded' (*dhimmi*), but a recognition of the comprehensive freedom of those who think differently and believe differently. The tolerance characteristic of modern culture is far more open than traditional Islamic tolerance. It recognizes people only as subjects at law with equal rights, regardless of their religion and origin; it cannot be divided up into citizens and those under their protection.

(c) *Secularity* in the sense of the recognition of autonomous spheres of life. What is meant is not the ideology of secularism, but 'secularity' as the freedom from religious supervision of such different spheres as economics, politics, law, and art. This freedom is one of the achievements of modern European culture and includes above all the separation of state and religion.

(d) *Democratic civil society* as a guarantor of a separation between the public and the private sphere which is safeguarded by the law and by institutions. Muslims enjoy the freedom to practise their religion publicly or privately, a freedom which is protected by the constitution. However, in the public arena of society they are citizens like anyone else, with no special rights.

(e) *Individual human rights.* Islam certainly has the concept of the *Haq adami*, a concept of human rights, but this has a completely different meaning from human rights as Europeans understand them. Human rights can be overridden by the law of God. Therefore Muslim declarations of human rights always stand under the proviso of the Shariah.

In this sense 'Euro-Islam' seeks to be the opposite of a ghetto Islam. Indeed, even more, it understands itself as a challenge, in the sense of rejecting a concept of ghetto Islam by exploiting the multiculturality of Europe. It regards itself as the only opportunity for the integration of Muslims into Europe, in that it makes the religious, spiritual and moral values of Islam compatible with the European history of freedom and constitutions. It does not want to isolate Muslims from the rest of society by exploiting the concept of multiculturality, but to integrate them into the pluralistic societies of Europe which already exist. Tibi associates with this the following expectation:

> If the Muslims living in Europe accept the foundations of modern Europe which have been set up, then they could become a religious community consisting of individuals as free citizens (thus not as a collective Umma) which – incidentally and indirectly – could serve as a model for the lands of their origin. Euro-Muslims could become advance posts of liberal reform and democracy in the relationship between East and West by appropriating modern culture. Otherwise there is a danger that the extremists, instead of contributing to an understanding between civilizations, will inflame the conflict between the civilizations. Regrettably there are already the disturbing beginnings of this, though they are not taken note of publicly.[12]

VI. The future of Islam in Europe is undecided

As a European Christian one follows the debates between Muslims on the future of Islam in Europe with the keenest attention, especially as parallels from the complex Christian history of the relationship between church and state immediately emerge. Just as it took centuries in the history of Christianity to establish a regulated relationship between church and state,

Euro-Islam: Challenge or Opportunity?

religion and society, politics and faith, which was relatively free of tension, so too long periods of assimilation will be needed in the history of modern Islam. The debate over the political and legal consequences of the substance of Islamic faith is far from having arrived at a consensus. The concept of 'Euro-Islam' is coming up against bitter resistance from Islamicist forces.

And yet we must note that movements have arisen, for example among the Islamic Associations in Germany after September 11 2001. Granted, no declaration by these movements, those by the Central Council of Muslims in Germany or by the Islamic Council, has ever adopted the concept of 'Euro-Islam' or even commented on it positively. But after an unprecedented anti-Islamic wave in Germany, too, after September 11 Muslims felt it necessary to communicate their own understanding of themselves better than before to the German and thus to the European public. This led to an Islamic Charta which was published in February 2002. It emphasizes that European history in the third millennium can no longer be written at the expense of Judaism or ignoring Islam:

> European culture resulted from the classical Hellenistic-Roman heritage, the Judeo-Christian-Islamic one, and the Enlightenment. In fact, European culture has been heavily influenced by Islamic philosophy and civilization. Also during the current transition from modernity to postmodernity Muslims are ready to contribute decisively to the overcoming of contemporary crises. This includes their Qur'anically demanded commitment to religious pluralism, their unconditional rejection of racism and chauvinism (no.14).

On the way in which Muslims understand themselves as citizens of their particular societies it is stated:

> Whether German citizens or not, the Muslims represented by the Central Council accept the basic legal order of the Federal Republic of Germany as guaranteed by its constitution, providing for the rule of law, division of power, and democracy, including a multi-party system, universal suffrage and eligibility, and freedom of religion. Therefore they accept as well everybody's right to change his religion, to have another religion, or none at all. The Qur'an forbids any compulsion or coercion in matters of faith (no.11).

> We do not aim at establishing a clerical theocracy. Rather we welcome the system existing in the Federal Republic of Germany where State and religion harmoniously relate to each other (no.12).

This declaration attracted great attention among the German public and must be understood as a signal of building trust. Even if the concept of 'Euro-Islam' is not to be found anywhere in it, it is possible to recognize a decided demarcation from the temptation to Islamic totalitarianism and an effort to accept the political and legal framework of European societies while at the same time living an authentic Muslim life. We may watch eagerly to see how the fundamental dispute between the traditional reactionary forces in Islam and the innovative forces orientated on the future will proceed in the European context.

Translated by John Bowden

Notes

1. Cf. B. Lyon et al., *Mohammed und Karl der Grosse. Die Geburt des Abendlandes* (with contributions by F. Gabriele, A. Guillou, B. Lyon, J. H. Pirenne and H. Steuer), Stuttgart and Zurich 1993.
2. F. Cardini, *Europa und der Islam. Geschichte eines Missverständnisses*, Munich 2000.
3. E. Horst, *Der Sultan von Lucera. Friedrich II. und der Islam*, Freiburg, Basle and Vienna 1997, p. 20.
4. Cf. K.-J. Kuschel, *Vom Streit zum Wettstreit der Religionen. Lessing und die Herausforderung des Islam*, Düsseldorf 1998. Also A. Hottinger, *Die Mauren. Arabische Kultur in Spanien*, Zurich 1995, ²1996; B. Brentjes, *Die Mauren. Der Islam in Nordafrika und Spanien*, Berlin and Leipzig ²1992.
5. M. Levy, *Die Sephardim in Bosnien. Ein Beitrag zur Geschichte der Juden auf der Balkanhalbinsel*, reprint of the 1911 edition, Klagenfurt 1996, p.150.
6. I. Lovrenović, *Bosnien und Herzegowina. Eine Kulturgeschichte*, Vienna and Bolzano 1998, p. 98.
7. J. Goytisolo, *Notizen aus Sarajevo*, Frankfurt am Main 1993, pp. 105f.
8. Id., *Kibla-Reisen in die Welt des Islam*, Frankfurt am Main 2000, p. 11.
9. Cf. U. Spuler-Stegemann, *Muslime in Deutschland. Nebeneinander oder Miteinander?*, Freiburg im Breisgau 1998.
10. Cf. K. Hafez (ed), *Der Islam und der Westen. Anstiftung zum Dialog*, Frankfurt am Main 1997.
11. Among my numerous publications on this topic see just those in: B. Tibi, *Im Schatten Allahs. Der Islam und die Menschenrechte*, Munich and Zurich 1994, pp. 298–314; id., *Europa ohne Identität? Die Krise der multikulturellen Gesellschaft*, Munich 1998, pp. 241–3; id., *Der Islam in Deutschland. Muslime in Deutschland*, Munich and Stuttgart 2000, pp. 325–49.
12. B.Tibi, *Im Schatten Allahs* (n.11), p.306.

III. Theological Challenge

Does Europe Jeopardize the De-Europeanization (and Purification) of the Church?

JAMES K. VOISS, SJ

Europe is in transition. Following two world wars and the decline of Communist socialism in Central and Eastern Europe, the European Union now seeks to fashion mutually beneficial bonds among the nations on the continent. It is a complex undertaking marked by sometimes conflicting values and values systems. This is perhaps most apparent in the realm of religion. Should religion have a place in the public discourse of the European Union? Should it exercise any influence in the life of the EU? It is possible to read the recent accession of countries with predominately Catholic populations such as Poland, Hungary, and Lithuania as signalling favourable responses to those questions. But when one considers how culturally and religiously pluralistic Europe has become since the middle of the twentieth century, especially with the influx of large non-Christian populations, such a response becomes less certain. Indeed, the tense discussion over whether or not to include reference to Europe's Christian history in the EU's constitution and the movement in France towards outlawing 'ostentatious religious symbols' in its public schools both underscore the ambiguous place of religion in the public life of the emerging Europe.

The possible influence of diverse religious sensibilities on the life of the European Union points to one aspect of the current complexity. But the question of influence also runs in the other direction. What impact might the EU have on religious institutions? This article makes that question more specific. Does Europe, or more specifically, does the forging of a transnational European identity in the EU, threaten to undermine a dynamism within the Roman Catholic Church toward de-europeanization?

The question is important. It touches on the relationship of church to state and culture, the nature of the church's identity and mission, and the internal dynamics of ecclesial life. Unfortunately, couching the question in terms of 'de-europeanization' is problematic, even misleading. It suggests that de-europeanization is a primary value for the church, somehow related to its purification. But whether it is a value, what it actually means, and how it stands in relationship to purification are far from clear. What follows will be an attempt to sort out these issues so as to provide a basis for assessing the role of Europe itself (if any) in the de-europeanization and purification of the church.

I. Why is 'de-europeanization' a question?

Prior to the Second Vatican Council, the spread of the Catholic Church throughout the world had, with few exceptions, meant the dissemination of European culture as the bearer and uniquely suitable form of expression of Western ecclesial Christianity. Latin worship, Gothic, romanesque, and baroque architecture, and European music exported to non-European contexts are among the most obvious external signs of the normative fusion between church and European culture.

This is not surprising. From the time of the Constantinian settlement, the church in Europe had maintained a symbiotic (if often uneasy) relationship with shifting governmental and economic forces on the continent. Indeed, the church *was* the lynch pin of European cultural identity, providing the common symbols which organized social life within and across linguistic and political boundaries. Consequently, when the late-fifteenth and sixteenth-century explorers exploded the horizons of the world beyond the North Atlantic and Mediterranean, the church's efforts to 'bring salvation' to the newly discovered peoples meant also bringing them European culture. The church implanted in these non-European cultures was thoroughly 'Europeanized'.[1]

By the mid-twentieth century, the fusion of church with European culture had collapsed. Several historical factors brought about its demise, among them, the fracturing of European Christianity in the Reformation, the intellectual heritage of the Enlightenment, and the emergence of Communist socialism in Central and Eastern Europe. European history had pushed the church to the margins of public discourse. The resulting critical distance between church and European culture led to the realization that the church exported to non-European cultures from Europe had imposed on those cultures what postmodern theorists would come to call hegemonic metanarratives of cultural superiority,[2] thereby perpetuating a form of injustice against those non-European cultures.

These shifting sensibilities led the church to re-examine its missionary strategies. De-europeanization names part of the post-conciliar missionary agenda. The imposition of europeanized Christianity on the non-European world had illegitimately suppressed legitimate cultural diversity in the name of the gospel. Some sort of corrective was required. De-europeanization seems an apposite name for that corrective. Is it?

II. Is 'de-europeanization' really the issue?

Since the Council, reflections on the relationship of the culturally European export church to the non-European world have developed under two headings: the world-church and inculturation. 'World-church' refers to a vision for the future of the church and describes a trajectory of development. Inculturation indicates the process(es) by which the church (world-church) comes to attain its culturally distinctive forms.

The German theologian Karl Rahner used the phrase world-church to name the theological significance of the Second Vatican Council.[3] At Vatican II, the church was no longer merely a 'European export' to the world. Rather, non-European bishops, native to the cultures in which they served, exercised a reciprocal (if limited) influence on the church's deliberations about its own nature and mission.[4] Rahner's reflections on this *de facto* occurrence argued that it signalled a definitive change in the self-realization of the church's nature. In a manner analogous to the relations among the patriarchates of the early church, regional churches in the world-church would exercise a reciprocal influence on each other. They would exercise this influence as relatively autonomous churches, always in union with the universal church, but having their own distinctiveness, reflecting their own cultural contexts.[5] That is, they would be inculturated churches.

Theological discussions of inculturation and world-church reflect similar aspirations for the future of the church. They envision a legitimate cultural, theological, and ecclesial pluralism. Unfortunately, the emphasis on pluriformity of ecclesial self-expression in both discussions can lead to the misconception that merely substituting non-European cultural forms for European ones will achieve an inculturated world-church. In fact, however, in both discussions, the pivotal concern lies elsewhere. Both discussions envision changes in external forms as a result of a change in the dynamics operative in the church's own life. That is, they presuppose the development of what might be termed a *communicative polycentrism* in the church. Europe would no longer function as the unique cultural centre or cultural resource for expressing ecclesial faith. Rather, as Rahner hoped, in a world-church, regional churches, under the leadership of their own bishops, would make decisions about how best to be church in their own distinctive cultural contexts. This would presumably result in non-European modes of ecclesial life, worship, and so on. But the pluriform expressions would be the consequence of a shift from culturally European mono-centrism (the presupposition for a culturally European export Christianity) to communicative polycentrism.

These developments would foster the emergence of the church *as* world-church. In such communicative polycentrism, non-European regional churches could mutually challenge and support each other (and the church in Europe) in how they express their ecclesial identity. But they would do so from within the forms of ecclesial self-expression most suited to their own local cultures. The communicative polycentrism at the basis of an inculturated world-church involves opening a space within the church in which the *other* (in this case, a non-European believing community) can be heard *as* other within the unity of the church. Non-European regional churches would not simply be the passive recipients of directives originating within an exclusively European cultural paradigm and presumed, as such, to be universally normative.[6]

The church in the United States reflects at a mesoscopic level the urgency and the complexity confronting the universal church on matters of communicative polycentrism and inculturation. As a nation of immigrants, Americans labour (not always successfully) to fashion a social unity that also respects (opens a space for) diversity of cultural heritage. American bishops face the same challenge. The tremendous influx of Hispanic/Latino Catholics in the United States has called into question the presumption that all American Catholics, regardless of cultural heritage, must somehow fit into an American church stamped by European cultural influences (i.e. Irish, Italian, German, and Polish). The sheer number of Hispanic/Latino American Catholics has lent pastoral urgency to inter-cultural dialogue within the American church. (Other groups such as African American, Vietnamese, and especially Native American Catholics, lacking the large numbers of the Hispanic/Latino populations, have occupied a less prominent place in such dialogues.) This inter-cultural conversation, opening the door to meaningful cultural adaptations of ecclesial life, is analogous to what the notion of communicative polycentrism intends.

'De-europeanization' attempts to name these complex issues. Certainly, fostering legitimate polycentrism in the church entails a diminishment of the European cultural hegemony which had been normative for so many centuries. But the term de-europeanization can mislead one into thinking that eradicating European influence and cultural forms is the primary objective. It is not. (Ironically, posing the question in terms of de-europeanization itself reflects the kind of eurocentric thinking that efforts to de-europeanize are presumably intended to overcome.) The primary issue is to change the dynamics of intra-ecclesial life. An inculturated world-church would change those dynamics in two significant ways. First, it would give non-Europeans an effective voice in shaping their own ecclesial life (within the unity of the one church). Second, it would empower non-European churches from their own ecclesial experiences of faith to reflect back to the universal church how it might more faithfully express its own nature, in both non-European and European contexts. This raises the question of purification.

III. What does de-europeanization have to do with purification of the church?

What does it mean to purify the church? Does it mean the restoration of the forms of ecclesial life dominant in the High Middle Ages? Does it mean Roman centralization in which the guarantee of purity is papal or Vatican sanction? Does it mean a simplistic cultural accommodationism and relativism? Does it mean excising all European influence from the church's self-expression in non-European regions of the world?

The Second Vatican Council chose none of these criteria for assessing the purification of the church. Indeed, it set no easily identifiable, static benchmark. Instead it opted to describe the purification of the church in terms of a dynamism of the Holy Spirit.[7] That dynamism envisioned by the Council is to be found at the intersection of three conciliar *verbi*: *aggiornamento* (bringing up to date), *ecclesia semper reformanda* (the church always in need of purification/reform), and the declaration that the church is in its nature a *sacrament*. All of the main documents of the Council can be read as efforts to update the church and initiate a process of on-going renewal *in order to enhance the church's credibility and effectiveness as sacrament to the world*. The yardstick the Council used to measure the purification was the adequacy of the church's self-expression as a 'sign and instrument, that is, of communion with God and of unity among all men [sic]' (*Lumen gentium* 1). As the Council phrased it, the church stands always in need of purification so that 'the sign of Christ may shine more brightly over the face of the Church' (*LG* 15; *Gaudium et spes* 43).[8]

Connecting the notion of purification to the dynamic sacramentality of the church as a whole has practical consequences. Improving sacramental efficacy presupposes, in the human scale, more effective communication. Effective communication requires commonly understood symbolic mediation (language, symbols, ritual actions, structures of social organization). In other words, the efficacy of the sacramental sign requires that those who receive it can recognize it for what it is. To draw people into its transformative dynamics more deeply, the church as sacramental sign must express itself in forms which individuals in distinctive cultures can engage. Purification of the sacrament-church *requires* inculturation.

Inculturating the church in diverse contexts is easier said than done. As Robert Schreiter has pointed out, it requires that one carefully negotiate the space between setting the church over against culture simply as critic of culture on the one hand and simplistic identification of the church with the local culture and all of its inherited forms on the other. Neither option is adequate.[9] Inculturation occurs in a process of communication in which the culture receiving the church is taken seriously as a co-conditioning, co-mediating partner with the universal church in the sacramental-communicative encounter.[10] The effectiveness of the church as sacrament in non-European cultures will to some degree be contingent on the universal (historically European) church's willingness to learn from the local culture what means of communication are most sacramentally effective for it at its particular point in time (*aggiornamento*) in that cultural context. And when the means initially employed are found by the church in a non-European culture to be less adequate than they might be for that context, they need to be re-purified (*ecclesia semper reformanda*), always with a view to greater sacramental efficacy. The dynamics of communication described here are what has been signalled above under the heading of a legitimate communicative polycentrism.

These reflections on purification and inculturation point to a further difficulty in the language of de-europeanization. The question in the title of this article implies that de-europeanization has an intrinsic connection to the purification of the church. De-europeanization entails the eradication or neutralization of European cultural impact on the self-expression of the church implanted in non-European cultural contexts. Thus, presumably, the church would become more pure the less it retains European cultural elements in non-European contexts.

While this formulation seems to echo the objectives of inculturation and to foster the world-church, in fact it distorts the issue at stake. As indicated above, inculturation is fundamentally about whether or not indigenous, non-European cultures are given any effective influence in how the church comes to realize itself within their own contexts. The issue is not simply European or non-European cultural forms. One non-European culture could legitimately decide that some aspects of European culture are better suited to expressing its ecclesial faith than the resources of its own local culture. Another non-European culture could, on that specific point, come to the opposite conclusion. Both would be inculturated expressions of the one church. The real issue is the degree to which the universal church supports and fosters local churches in non-European contexts in finding the most adequate ways of making the church to be an effective sacramental sign within the distinctive (non-European) cultural context.

IV. What role does Europe play?

This article has argued that the language of de-europeanization is a limited, and potentially misleading way of naming the post-conciliar interest in promoting an inculturated world-church. It has identified communicative polycentrism as the essential dynamism both for inculturation and for the on-going purification of the sacrament-church called for by the Council. One question now remains. Does Europe – specifically the emerging European Union – jeopardize the development of such an ecclesial polycentrism? A brief response will have to suffice.

It is unlikely that the emerging Europe will exercise direct influence on the internal workings of the church. The symbiotic synthesis between church and European culture prior to the Reformation that gave rise to a 'europeanized' export church no longer exists. Both the cultural and religious pluralism within the member states of the European Union, and the Catholic Church's own teaching on religious freedom present obstacles to that synthesis ever being reconstituted. Moreover, present-day Europe – even now in the process of forging its new identity – appears to be ambivalent about any identification with the religious symbols of the past (much to John Paul II's distress).[11] Europe, as an emerging corporate reality, is not concerned with the internal life of the church. It therefore does not appear to threaten the de-europeanization, purification, or emergence of communicative polycentrism within the church.

Nevertheless, the future of ecclesial communicative polycentrism (de-europeanization) is far from secure. Not everyone within the church agrees that the polycentrism discussed here should be promoted. Some regard the pluralism that would result as a threat to another important ecclesial value, visible unity within the church. In the period since the Council, the intra-ecclesial tension generated by these competing values has not yet been resolved, although the balance is currently tipped towards the emphasis on visible unity. Thus, during the pontificate of John Paul II, decision-making authority has been heavily centralized, concentrated in the hands of Roman curial officials. It is important to note that the distinctive ecclesial culture of the Roman curia is not identical with European culture. Nevertheless, it is decidedly European, owing much to both the historical synthesis of church and culture of an earlier age and the European heritage and/or training of many of its most influencial members. As a result, the concentration of decision-making authority in the hands of Roman curial officials has two effects relevant to the present discussion. First, it reinforces a kind of European cultural dominance within the church. Second, it militates against the communicative polycentrism discussed here.[12] It is this intra-ecclesial centralization of decision-making authority, not the emergence of the European Union, which jeopardizes the de-europeanization of the church.

Notes

1. For a succinct overview of this situation see, Karl Rahner, 'Rites Controversy: New Tasks for the Church' in *Human Society and the Church of Tomorrow*, in *Theological Investigations 22*, New York: Crossroad 1991, p. 134.
2. For an overview of the critique of metanarratives, see Stanley J. Grenz, *A Primer on Postmodernism*, Grand Rapids: Eerdmans 1996, pp. 42–46. Lieven Boeve explores some of the theological implications of this critique in 'Critical Consciousness in the Postmodern Condition: New Opportunities for Theology?' *Philosophy and Theology* 10, no. 2 (1997), pp. 449–68.
3. Karl Rahner, 'Basic Theological Interpretation of the Second Vatican Council' in *Concern for the Church*, in *Theological Investigations 20*, London: Darton, Longman & Todd 1981 presents Rahner's seminal treatment of the world-church. For further discussion see, in the same volume, 'The Abiding Significance of the Second Vatican Council' and 'The Future of the Church and the Church of the Future'.
4. Karl Rahner, 'Basic Theological Interpretation', pp.78–80.
5. See Karl Rahner, 'The Future of the Church and the Church of the Future', pp. 110–11; Rahner, 'Basic Theological Interpretation', pp.78–79.
6. Such a shift in operation provokes resistance, as Rahner himself recognized. See his discussion in Rahner, 'Rites Controversy', p. 135.
7. See, for example, 'Gaudium et spes' in *Vatican Council II: The Conciliar and Post Conciliar Documents* ed. Austin Flannery, Northport, NY: Costello 1975), pp. 21, 38, 43.

Does Europe Jeopardize the De-Europeanization of the Church? 85

8. As found in *LG* 15, the phrase refers to the need for the members of the church to undergo purification so that they may give more credible witness to the light of Christ. The application in *GS* is much broader, signalling the need for the whole church to undergo purification so as to give better witness to the Gospel it proclaims. The Council saw no opposition between the two. Purification of the lives of the members issues in purification of the visible presentation of the church. Purification of the church leads to purification of the members. The Council seemed to recognize a reciprocal relationship here.
9. Robert Schreiter, 'Inculturation of Faith or Identification with Culture?' in *Christianity and Cultures: A Mutual Enrichment* ed. Norbert Greinacher and Norbert Mette, *Concilium*, Maryknoll, NY: Orbis Books and London: SCM Press 1994, pp. 15–24, esp. p. 23 Similar tensions arise when discussing the world-church. See, for example, Avery Dulles, 'The Emerging World Church: A Theological Reflection' in *Proceedings of the Catholic Theological Society of America*, vol. 39, ed George Kilcourse, Washington, DC: Catholic Theological Society of America 1984, pp.1–12.
10. On criteria for inculturation see Robert J. Schreiter, *Constructing Local Theologies*, Maryknoll, NY: Orbis and London: SCM Press 1985, pp. 117–21.
11. John Paul II, 'Ecclesia in Europa,' *Origins* 33, no. 10 (2003), esp. pp. 7, 24, and 110.
12. On these two points, recent criticism of Roman curial practices by the former Superior General of the Carmelites, Camilo Macisse, is instructive. See Camilo Macisse, 'Violence in the Church', *The Tablet*, 22 November 2003, pp. 8–9

A European Civil Religion?

GIUSEPPE RUGGIERI

I. Towards understanding the present situation

The Christian churches feel deeply involved in the process of constructing a European unity which is increasingly integrated not only at an economic level but also at a political level. This interest of the churches in Europe cannot be explained solely by contingent motives. In the Christian faith, almost from the time of Paul, there has been almost a natural drive to overcome the confines of peoples and nations. Indeed the motif of the universal redemption offered in Christ, so that there is neither Greek nor barbarian, but all are one in Christ, itself constitutes a dialectical principle with respect to the bonds which unite a people and distinguish it from other peoples. The principle of the unity of all women and all men in Christ is not formally opposed to all the various distinctions introduced through history. It puts the unity at a level which is radically different from the cultural, political and juridical level. However, one can only welcome with open arms any social and political order which tends to abolish barriers.

If we move on from these abstract and ideal reflections to concrete history, things appear more complex. In the one hand, in its more radical manifestations faith has been and is the inspiration of criticisms of the existing order of the world, which is judged to be ephemeral, if not contrary to God's design, because of the internal and external divisions of individuals and people. On the other hand, at least since the time when peace was established between Christianity and the later Roman empire, a peace which continued even when the barbarians became the heirs of the Roman empire, Christian universalism has given birth, above all in the Middle Ages, to a transnational community, Christendom, distinct both from the church and from individual states, but endowed with its own unity, with laws and customs that were generally recognized. Christendom inevitably had its enemies at that time,[1] since the unity which it represented was of a cultural, legal and political kind, often antithetical to the unity which the gospel of the kingdom promises to all women and men.

A European Civil Religion?

In the West this Christendom was formally abolished when the two revolutions, the French and American revolutions, declared that the state was not competent to enact laws 'respecting an establishment of religion or prohibiting the free exercise thereof' (First Amendment of the Constitution of the United States of America), or stated the principle that 'no one has the right to be troubled for his opinions, even religious opinions, provided that their expression does not disturb the public order established by the law' (Article 10 of the Declaration of the Rights of Man and the Citizen). If we look carefully, we can see that the formulae of the two constitutions have a common feature: the laws are declared so to speak indifferent to religious convictions. That brought down the fundamental pillar of Christianity.

Even here, however, history seems more complex. Mediaeval Christendom has in fact in some way survived down to our own day, despite the separation between the churches introduced in the West by the Protestant Reformation and despite its formal dissolution in the new situation created by modern revolutions. It survives in fact in remnants (traces of legislation and customs), or as an ideal, and not only for Catholics. The thousand years of interpenetration between the demands of the Christian faith and social laws has left an indelible mark on the culture of the European peoples.

On the other hand, these survivals of Christianity have to take into account the process of secularization in the West, a process that some want to derive finally from the conception of the world present in the Jewish-Christian tradition and that others oppose to it. Secularization has created an objectively new situation both for Christendom and for the churches.[2] Even before the term 'secularization' blossomed in the course of the treaties of the Peace of Westphalia in 1646, in which it was used to indicate the expropriation of ecclesiastical property in favour of the princes or the national Reformed churches, it appeared in the canonical disputes at the end of the sixteenth century to indicate the passage of a religious from the regular state to the secular state. It should be noted that this origin is not just an erudite fact, a curiosity; it is essential to note it if one is to understand the concept and the historical views that it conveys. 'From the time of its first emergence the term secularization therefore seems part of an antithetical scheme: it already contains within itself, though only virtually, a dualism of that regular and secular which is the modern metamorphosis of the Pauline contrast between heavenly and earthly, contemplative and active, spiritual and worldly.'[3] In present-day thinking therefore the term evokes not only the process by which the church's control of social life weakened, whether because of its loss of possession and control of particular goods; or because of institutional changes in the relationship between church and society; or because of changes of mentality, but also a view of the relationship between church and society which corresponds with our contemporary situation.

However, the framework of secularization cannot be reduced to the description I have just given. In fact, as some scholars have taken the trouble to note, it has never done away with the religious dimension of social life but has kept it in the form of 'civil religion'. To go back to the distant origins of this concept, we have to refer to Terentius Varro (died 27 BCE), a writer used by Augustine. For Varro, a 'civil theology' is necessary for the administration of the city.[4] However, Rousseau, not Varro, is the author to whom people today refer.[5] And in fact it was the American Robert Bellah who revived Rousseau's concept of civil religion, though he used it to cover not only the religious truths necessary to the conduct of the state but also the fundamental values of a community, its vision of the world.[6] The term 'civil religion' takes on different specific meanings in different national and European contexts,[7] but Rousseau's formulations have been long lived, and still possess a clarity which those who refer to him sometimes lack:

> There is a purely civil profession of faith[8] the articles of which are fixed by the sovereign; not, however, as religious dogmas but as *sentiments of sociability* (my emphasis), without which it would be impossible to be a good citizen or a faithful subject. The sovereign cannot force anyone to believe; however, a person can be banished by the state as being incapable of standing in society (French '*insociable*'), of sincerely loving the laws and justice, and of sacrificing, if need be, his own life for his duty.[9]

However, much attention needs to be paid to one point, over and above the varieties of the use of civil religion in various national or continental contexts (the United States has in fact experimented with a relationship between religion and society which is very different from that of the European peoples). Civil religion cannot indicate the political relevance which each religion inevitably possesses, whether conservative or revolutionary. So it is not synonymous with 'political atheism', 'political Christianity', and so on. In fact a religion could be politically very relevant, even if was rejected by the whole of a society. Rather, as H. Lübbe has rightly noted, it is important to understand that civil religion is given by

> the totality of the stable elements of religious culture which are in fact integrated into the political situation, or even formally and institutionally, as in the case of the religious law of the state. So these elements are not entrusted to the religious communities as their specific concern, but,

without prejudicing the religious freedom that is guaranteed, bind the citizens to the (civil) community even in their religious existence and independently of their membership of a confession. Therefore they represent this civil community itself, in its institutions and its representatives, as being in the last resort legitimated by a religion, and therefore also recognized for religious motives.[10]

The evolution of Western society has also introduced a variant into the concrete dynamic of civil religion. Although the values of civil religion are not in fact peculiar to the church, in the fragmentation caused by the evolution of post-industrial cultures no one is better capable than the churches at demonstrating that they are nourished by these values. The churches have therefore recognized their function in a new way, particularly in those secularized societies which no longer accept their control and remain preoccupied with maintaining religious plurality and freedom. Nothing is more eloquent here than the words addressed by the Bavarian *Kultusminister* to the Catholic theologians of Europe on the occasion of the official reception during their second congress, in Monaco, on 30 August 1995:

What is the significance of the faith and the church today? Despite a diagnosis which would seem more to suggest that these are illusions which are disappearing, in my view it is wrong to write them off. In my opinion, to the degree that politicians are aware of their own responsibilities in this situation, they will think it sensible and necessary to defend the strong position of the two great Christian confessions in our country, not only in the interest of the church but rather because it is also in the interest of our state. What the state guarantees all churches, from legal protection to economic support, is not in fact an act of beneficence towards them. If we reflect a little, we will note that by acting in this way the state is doing a 'favour' to itself. It is evident that the churches, yesterday as today, constitute very important factors of integration into our society and our state. They in fact stabilize political culture, handing on value and a sense of value to a large number of men and women. In this way they not only give support to individuals but also form a counterbalance to the increasingly pronounced individualization and atomization of our societies.[11]

Strangely heterogeneous aims are presented here: the churches are invited to function in the dynamic of society and meet the demands for its civil cohesion, but they are to do so for their own ends. It is obvious that church and civil society (and the state which expresses it) act with opposite intentions. On the part of the church there is a desire not to be reduced to a social function; a claim that its own mission is original and irreducible, and that its own presence is not based on a treaty and political changes but on the divine foundation of the one who rules the church itself, a conviction that human beings are created by God and ordained for him, and all this plays a part every dimension of the context in which the church legitimately operates. The influence in the dynamics of civil society which is sought is seen as being a consequence of a mandate received from Christ himself.

On the other side, there is a tendency to ignore this 'claim'. A modern secular state is based on a treaty between citizens which is laid down in its constitution; it recognizes their religious convictions *de facto*, to the degree that these do not prejudice the convictions of the other parties to the treaty. The secular state for its part (and the public opinion of our contemporary societies), while rejecting the elements of conflict which inevitably arise from the religious diversity of its citizens and therefore the absoluteness in which the conflict itself is always rooted, recognizes the function that the substance of the beliefs plays in guaranteeing peace between citizens. Even care for the poor and the proclamation of solidarity in fact serve as a decompression chamber whch makes the social disparities tolerable. This is a very important function in the control of collective violence which, if not the only aim, is certainly one of the aims of the state itself.

It is in the light of all this that the request often made by the current bishop of Rome for a remembrance of the Christian roots of Europe to be included in the European constitution is to be understood. From a historical point of view this is a quite legitimate, if unilateral, claim. The influence of Christianity (and thus of its Jewish origins) on the formation of Europe, including modern Europe, is undeniable, though it cannot be denied that other factors were operative that cannot be reduced to Christianity, like Arab culture in the Middle Ages or the totality of modern values, often said to be contrary to historical Christianity though not to the gospel (Rousseau himself made this distinction in the text which I quoted above). But a constitution is not a historical text, and the problem for the European Constitution is not that of reconstructing the history of Europe.

To sum up, the substance of the problem which arises could be put like this: how is the recognition, *de facto* or formal, of the role that the churches have played in maintaining a 'civil religion' of citizens to be assessed?

II. The challenge to the faith of the churches

I believe that in a situation which is even more complex than I have attempted to describe, the task of the theologian is first of all to discern what issues are in fact at stake. The scenario which opens up in the present situation does not depend on the formal insertion of a remembrance of the Christian roots of Europe into the text of the new European Constitution. Over and beyond this episode, which is ultimately irrelevant, the concrete evolution of relations between the Christian faith and European society has in fact produced an alternative which runs through the whole history of the church, at least from the fourth century on.[12] What is arising now is only a new expression of the difficulties which the churches have always had in maintaining their particular eschatological dimension, their prime and constitutive relationship with the gospel of the kingdom. So if the churches allow themselves to be integrated into the dynamics of civil society, to serve the ends that these societies historically present, it is less and less improbable that they will succeed in bringing out the radical difference between the kingdom of God and the dynamic of human societies. In that case the message they bear will tend to abandon the dimension of the gospel and assume that of the ethical value.

I cannot enter here into the merits of the discussion on 'values', on whether or not they are objectively transcendent in respect of the knowledge of the subject, whether or not they constitute an experience which can be reduced to a moral experience, and so on. However, from my point of view it is essential to state that in our society the 'value' has taken the place of the notion of good, and designates what is *now* capable of motivating the action of a person or a social group. If we want to understand the dynamic of our society, we are forced to accepted the sociological reduction of values practised by Max Weber.[13] The transcendence of values is only 'normative', i.e. it is that which allows them to become terms of reference for concrete and historical human action, independent of their intrinsic validity. The priority which is now given to the dimension of values rather than to that of the good in fact implies a recognition of the priority of 'evaluating' on the part of human beings.

Today societies do not value the social utility of the churches in the same way as they did in the past. A climate of opposition has given way to a more tranquil symbiosis. Even in secularized societies the churches make a marked contribution towards supporting those values which these societies need for their equilibrium in pursuing the aims that they set themselves. But the churches must be aware that in accepting this role, indeed pursuing it, they must also accept the corresponding translation of the message of the gospel and its integration into a dynamic which is extraneous to it. So they have to choose the means of serving men and women which most corresponds to their vocation to announce the kingdom and construct a 'religious' city.

The problem can be described by means of an alternative: on the one hand the church accepts being configured publicly in such a way as to make visible the logic of the gospel; but on the other hand it accepts being configured as a support in pursuing the goals of a particular society. Realistically there is a need to accept that it is very difficult for the churches to withdraw themselves from the recognition offered them by a democratic or substantially secularized society. This is a new and unprecedented form of a very ancient alliance. At least from the fourth century on, when it became a mass religion, Christianity has performed the function played in Israel by the 'religion of the fathers', and within the Roman empire by traditional 'pagan religion'.

It is also true that as a result of this recognition the churches can often also defend the rights of the victims of the societies in which they are situated. But realistically it has to be recognized that this alliance is the source of suffering and unease for those who remain sensitive to what Vatican II (*Lumen gentium* 8.3) calls the way of Jesus, the obligatory way of the gospel which is that of poverty, humility and abnegation. This way of Jesus is not necessarily hostile to the demands of human co-existence, which are also those of civil religion, but the preoccupation of Christians who want to follow the way of Jesus is to bring out the positive character of the kingdom of God which is always coming in history, above all to the victims of society who are seeking that God who, as the Psalmist said, 'trains my hand for war, so that my arms can bend a bow of bronze' (Ps.18.35). With no less realism than those who accept the function of Christianity as a civil religion, those who are preoccupied with the purity of the gospel note the inevitable lapses to which the churches are subject when they are seeking to render to God what Caesar wants.

Confronted with this alternative, which still runs through the life of the churches, we should perhaps just limit ourselves to remembering the responsible suffering of Francis of Assisi, who in his *Testament* (1226) reminded the brothers of the need to be faithful to the form of the gospel and at the same time to recognize the validity of the form of the Roman church. Here, too, in fact history shows how the attempt to raise one form against another like a battle standard, making the realistic compromise of a church preoccupied with its social recognition, contrary to the authority of discipleship along the way of Jesus, and vice versa, ultimately ignores the gospel of mercy.

Certainly it is possible to write an 'ideal' theology and try to show the need for a 'church of the people' on the one hand and the demand of evangelical radicalism on the other. The former can claim the undeniable measure of realism, the latter the lucid coherence of faithfulness to origins. I think that I have shown clearly which I think to be true. But I prefer the humility of Francis's position to the hypocrisy of forced justifications or the hybris of intolerant purity.

Translated by John Bowden

Notes

1. Cf. G. Ruggieri (ed), *I nemici della cristianità*, Bologna 1997.
2. H.-W. Strätz, 'Wegweiser zur Säkularisation in der kanonistischen Literatur' in A. Rauscher (ed), *Säkularisierung und Säkularisation vor 1800*, Paderborn 1976; id., 'Die Säkularisation und ihre nächsten staatskirchenrechtlichen Folgen' in A.Langner (ed), *Säkularisation und Säkularisierung im 19. Jahrhundert*, Munich and Paderborn 1978; id., 'Säkularisation, Säkularisierung II' in *Geschichtliche Grundbegriffe. Historisches Lexikon zur politisch-sozialen Sprache in Deutschland* V, Stuttgart 1984.
3. G. Marramao, *Cielo e terra. Genealogia della secolarizzazione*, Bari 1994, p. 17, with references to the studies by Strätz.
4. Varro distinguished between 'mythical' theology, i.e. knowledge of God which expresses itself in fables, a mode to which poets resort; 'natural' theology, to which philosophers resort without knowing how to distinguish true from false; and 'civil' theology, which citizens, and especially priests, should know and administer in cities: M. Terentius Varro, *Antiquitates rerum divinarum*, fr. 9, ed B. Cardauns, Mainz and Wiesbaden 1976.
5. Cf. J. J. Rousseau, *Du contrat social* ed M. Halbwachs, Paris 1943, Book IV, chapter 8.
6. From Bellah's vast literary production I mention simply 'Civil Religion in America', *Daedalus* 96, 1967, pp. 1–21, and *The Broken Covenant. American Civil Religion in Time of Trial*, New York 1975; for a synthetic work cf. R. Schieder, *Civil Religion. Die religiöse Dimension der politischen Kultur*, Gütersloh 1987. Note that this author prefers not to translate Bellah's American term.
7. See the recent issue of *Theologische Quartalschrift* 183/2, 2003, dedicated to civil religion and edited by R. Puza. This takes into consideration the contexts of France, Hungary, Germany, Belgium, the Netherlands and Italy.
8. The expression 'civil' faith was already present in Voltaire. Rousseau used 'civil faith' and 'civil religion' indiscriminately.

9. Rousseau, *Contrat social* (n. 5), p. 427.
10. H. Lübbe, 'Staat und Zivilreligion. Ein Aspekt politischer Legitimität' in H. Kleger and A. Müller (eds), *Religion des Bürgers. Zivilreligion in Amerika und Europa*, Munich 1986, p. 206.
11. Quoted from the French edition of the speech distributed to those present. In my possession.
12. For what follows see G. Ruggieri, *Cristianesimo chiese e vangelo*, Bologna 2002, pp. 339–58.
13. Max Weber, 'Der Sinn der Wertfreiheit der soziologischen und ökonomischen Wissenschaften', *Logos. Internationale Zeitschrift für Philosophie und Kultur* 7, 1917, pp. 40–88.

Christianity in a Multi-Religious Europe

THOMAS BREMER

I. Europe has always been multi-religious

Europe has always been multi-religious. It is no new phenomenon that adherents of other religions in Europe are present alongside Christianity in its various forms. The Christianization of the continent took many centuries, in which forms of pre-Christian religions and syncretism were to be found almost everywhere, and even before it was completed there were Jews and Muslims in various parts of Europe. But the divisions within Christianity must also be noted: the separation between the Christian East and the West after the eleventh century; the various movements of the high Middle Ages; and the Reformations of the sixteenth century, which also brought about a diversity in the European religious landscape. Even before the expulsions of Jews and Muslims, adherents of these religions appeared in south-eastern Europe, and although the presence of Islam in Albania and Bosnia would not have been brought into public awareness without the wars and unrest of the 1990s, both religions have a tradition there going back over centuries. Turkey, the compatibility of whose membership of the EU is being discussed, was for a long time a significant European power. Finally, the migrations of modernity have contributed to religions from the Far East and Africa also being represented almost everywhere in Europe. In Hamburg alone, a city traditionally stamped by Lutheranism, there are more than fifty different black African communities and churches[1] – one indication that traditional religious milieus hardly still exist.

So Europe has always been multi-religious. Nevertheless Europe has been and is regarded as *the* Christian continent. As is well known, Christianity became the predominant religion in Europe, so that while the other religions were present, they were always regarded as marginal phenomena. The Christian churches have largely succeeded over history in presenting themselves as the only legitimate, because the only true, religion. This exclusivism also applied to other rival forms of Christianity, and only gradually after the Peace of Westphalia in 1648 were the main churches compelled to recognize, by no means willingly and out of insight, that they had to co-exist, though without accepting that other Christian bodies were churches and without rejecting persecution of and discrimination against smaller Christian groups and churches. The stabilization of Christianity in Europe by its association with ruling structures made a decisive contribution not only to its becoming the predominant religion on the European continent but also to the fact that where Christian rulers were in power the areas which they controlled were regarded as (or made) Christian. In this way the continent generally adopted the Christian faith. A quite similar phenomenon can also be observed in Islam; particularly at the points of contact between the two religions, about all in south-east Europe, we can see very clearly where the two claims competed with one another in history: if areas changed from Austrian to Ottoman rule they were no longer 'Christian', and vice versa. The specific religious practice of the population did not play any great role here. However, in central Europe the ruling structures and frontiers remained intact; at any rate they could not come under non-Christian control, and so Europe was and remained Christian. The actual presence of other religions was marginalized – either in respect of Islam in southern Europe, which lay 'on the periphery' of Europe, or within society, where other religions were sometimes tolerated when practised by individuals if that seemed opportune for various reasons, for example in the case of Jews.

II. Colonies and missionaries

With the discovery and conquest of other continents this situation changed. The European states now had colonies in which the majority of the population was not Christian. Missionary work among these 'heathen' went hand in hand with the conquest of the territories concerned and the consolidation of rule over them. Here the colonial states co-operated closely with the majority churches. Thus initially an awareness of the problem did not arise; however, interest in the religion of the areas concerned increased, and in academic theology disciplines like religious studies and mission studies gradually came into being. So Europe as *the* Christian part of the earth strove (in many cases successfully) to export Christianity to the rest of the world. Initially the other religions were not taken seriously as conversation partners, nor can there even be talk of tolerance towards them, but their existence was noted. This concern to a considerable degree contributed to the possibility of the non-Christian religions in Europe moving from being an object of contemplation to being the subject of dialogue. Whereas until well into the twentieth century careers in the European mother countries were possible only for those colonials who had largely adapted in life-style, education and religion, the adoption of the Christian religion by people who did not take on any leadership functions was thought not to be necessary. The result was that more and more Muslims, Sikhs and others came to Europe. The reinforcement of the missionary movement in the years after 1945, which has already been mentioned, was another factor.

The recognition that Europe was increasingly ceasing to be a Christian continent was an often wearisome and painful progress, especially for the main Christian churches. They had to watch their once unassailed position being threatened more and more. But at the same time they gradually developed an understanding of the value and necessity of inter-religious dialogue. Thus the present situation – for all its difficulties and defects – differs considerably from that of past centuries. For the first time we can see different religions living together in a way which is not primarily based on competition and reduced to the conviction that the others must also be made adherents of one's own religion. The diversity of religions is a fact with which in the meantime the representatives of the traditional religions have also come to terms; indeed they can sometimes see the positive side of it.

III. The theology of religions

What does this mean for Christianity and theology? In principle Christianity makes the claim that its explanation of God and the world is the only true one, that it is also valid for all those people who do not know Christianity or reject it. This conviction must necessary clash with the mere existence of other manifestations of religion. It can make sense only if the other religions in some way point to Christianity and the Christian God. This view is expressed in the documents of Vatican II,[2] and is in tension with the theology of religions, especially its more recent developments, which not only allow the other religions a value of their own but understand them as being in some way parallel to Christianity. This has also provoked doctrinal statements from Rome in recent years.

It should be noted that concrete circumstances, contexts, not only shape theological modes of expression but are also the occasion for theological insights. That means not only that the Christian churches in Europe must reflect pastorally and theologically on the presence of other religions, but that this presence also challenges the Christian claim to absoluteness. The other religions must be given their own place in the thought of Christianity. That calls for a long and intensive process of theological thought, and just as the question raised by the theology of religions has not yet been settled, so too this challenge will not find a clear answer which satisfies everyone. Nevertheless the European churches face the necessity of now finding ways of dealing with the other religions, not only tolerating them in practice but also adopting theological approaches towards their integration into the understanding of European Christianity. This task is all the more urgent since the churches are in some respects entangled in the disastrous European history of relations with other religions, so that here too they must take some historical responsibility.

How can the churches appropriately assume this responsibility? A first and necessary step is to accept the *de facto* presence of the other religions in 'Christian' Europe by perceiving them as they are and in their otherness and not tolerating them at best as alien phenomena. However, here the result of the theological discussion which is needed must not be anticipated. First of all, then, the churches must take note of the other religions in Europe. That can happen in many ways. A first step is to get to know them. Often members of the traditional churches and other churches and religious communities live side by side without knowing much of each others' traditions of faith and religious practices. Experience shows that such processes can and must be guided. So an active approach towards one another is necessary. Here it is important that encounters and contacts are not just limited to the level of church governments and the leaders of non-Christian religious communities, but also include believers. They must get to know one another's religious convictions and practices. At the same time the representatives of the other faith communities must be shown that they are not felt to be alien bodies, but that their presence represents an enrichment of the European religious landscape. That can come about especially by practical action, especially as the question of places for these communities to meet and pray is often a problem over which the mainstream churches could help them. In providing such places the churches would also be bearing witness to how Christians in the modern world should deal with other religions. Such service is more convincing than any words. Here the Christian attitude must not be dependent on how great the openness and tolerance is on the other side. The Christian imperative to love one's neighbour which must be tested here is not negated if the neighbour does not accept the offer of dialogue or has other principles. Clearly the principles of Christian faith cannot be put in question in this way. Dialogue with other religions does not mean adopting their value systems; on the contrary, in this way Christianity can demonstrate its own values and put them into practice.

Here, then, are some principles for the interrelationship of the religions in Europe. There remains the question of its theological significance. To exaggerate somewhat, we can ask: what does it mean for salvation if Islam, various Asian religions, Judaism and many other manifestations of religion in Europe are not only represented by individual believers but can establish their presence and even gain adherents among people who were originally Christian or had no religious beliefs? What ways are there for the Christian churches to deal theologically with this challenge?

Theologically, the question is decided by what basic attitude is adopted to the problems discussed by the theology of religions. It is dependent on the significance for salvation attributed to other religions. If the assumption is that they have none, then their presence in Europe can have no significance either. In that case they are in fact an alien body which at best can be tolerated. On such presuppositions active dialogue and lively exchange are inconceivable. Even if we were to assume that the presence of the others in Europe represents (only) a challenge to Christianity, in principle the fact remains that they would not be vehicles of a value of their own; they would not be subjects, but objects and instruments, the ultimate purpose of which would consist in a revival of the Christian tradition.

However, things are different if the other religions are not only regarded as a challenge (which beyond doubt they are) but are also given a value of their own. Europe is the continent which has been stamped by the co-existence of various languages, nations, cultures and also religions. The presence of the non-Christian religions is at the same time due to the special character of Europe, because diversity and co-existence are part of its essence. The logic that Christian Europe accepts people of other religious convictions and offers them a home entails that it also respects and allows the religion of these people. Tolerance of them is not only a social necessity, nor is it due solely to the pressure of facts. It is an intrinsic part of Christianity, regardless of Christianity's claim to offer the 'correct' interpretation of the world. For a long time this consciousness did not exist, and as I have indicated above, it has developed through the real presence of the other religions. But that does not change the fact that it is intrinsically right. The contextuality of the religious situation in Europe has resulted in the churches becoming aware of the need of dialogue with others; this is one example of how the religious context can create new insights which then are nevertheless fully justified and valid.

IV. The question of Christianity in multi-religious Europe

Thus it is evident that the real situation in Europe offers a pattern of interpretation which can contribute towards recognizing the value of the religions which on the continent traditionally had to be regarded as minority religions. This has made it possible for the different forms of Christianity, as the faith communities of the majority, to recognize the other religions as others, i.e. to perceive them in their independence and see this as a value which does not necessarily put the Christian world-view in question but in some circumstances can even supplement it or complete it. It is obvious that here the monotheistic religions of Judaism and Islam play a special role, not only because of their historical significance for and in Europe but also and above all because of the theological challenge which they pose with their proximity to Christianity but also their emphatic differences. For the same reasons, conversely, this must also be a special interest for the Christian churches in encountering these two religions and their representatives in Europe. Above all in the case of Islam, it is evident that this encounter also has eminently political connotations.

The question of Christianity in multi-religious Europe has one further dimension. Europe was and is regarded as the 'Christian' continent. But in fact it is the case that not only have phenomena of secularization made themselves clear in the Christian churches of Europe with a greater intensity than almost anywhere else, but that as a result of the increase in numbers of adherents of the other religions, these are gaining more and more importance, and that the traditional Christian confessions are losing not only members but social influence. In some areas, especially in the big cities, the non-traditional religious forms have quantitatively already surpassed the traditional ones. That too is a challenge for the Christian churches, since in 'their' own territories they could find themselves in a minority situation. For the first time they are facing rivals who – because of the principles of modern free political systems – enjoy the same freedom and privileges as they do and are thus in a situation of public competition with the churches. That this is at least in part the case already becomes clear from the fact that numerous people who come from a Christian tradition are turning to another, non-European religion. The phenomenon of the growing significance of esotericism should also be mentioned in this context.

So here is a further challenge for the churches. The foreign mission which Europe has engaged in for centuries will now be necessary at home – in quite a different way. The term 'mission on all continents'[3] was coined at a very early stage of the ecumenical movement. Now more than ever the significance of this way of thinking is becoming evident in reality. Europe is still a 'Christian' continent (or better a continent with a Christian stamp), but more than ever that will inevitably change.

Finally, mention should be made of Christian theology. The situation depicted here has far-reaching consequences for it also. It can no longer start from an inner Christian European perspective but has to formulate its statements in the context of the presence of other religions. The experiences of mission studies, ecumenical theology and contextual theology will certainly come into their own here. A structural change in institutionalized theology and an intensive grappling with religious studies has already begun in many countries; in others it has still to happen, but there too it will be unavoidable. The consequences for traditional Christian theology are unforeseeable.

V. A few theses

I shall sum up in a few theses, with brief explanations, the most important results of these reflections.

1. Europe is the continent which is most strongly marked by great ethnic, religious, linguistic, political and cultural diversity in a relatively small area, so that here basically there is also a tradition of religious pluralism.

Diversity in every respect is virtually a key characteristic of the European continent. It has led to numerous conflicts and tensions, but also to the rise of toleration, though in a long and often painful process. Even when practical or political necessities have often been in the foreground here, the result is the development of diverse societies which can live alongside each other and with each other peacefully.

2. The Christian churches and their theologies have taken a long time to perceive the value of the presence of other religions in Europe other than as a threat, but they have made a contribution to the development of toleration.

Because of the claim of Christianity to absoluteness, other religions have traditionally been regarded as non-religions, as false convictions. An awareness of the value of these religions has arisen only at a very late stage in Christianity. This made it possible to move from confrontation and a sense of mission to dialogue. In this way the church has contributed to an encounter with other religions. Here the previous disastrous history of these contacts must not be concealed.

3. This presence represents not only a challenge but also an opportunity for Christianity. It can show in a new way how the missionary impulse can be dealt with.

It has become evident in the history of Christian mission that through a preoccupation with other religions an understanding of them has grown, so that it has been possible, for example, for contextual Christian theologies to develop. It has become evident that the Christian churches also needed mission in the lands from which the missionaries came. Through the presence of the other religions in Europe these impulses from mission theology can be made fruitful in Europe as well.

4. The questions raised by the theology of religions need a well-thought out answer, so that the attitude of Christianity in Europe towards the other religions can be established.

In principle the relationship of the Christian churches to the other religions depends on what value the churches put on them. The critical question which is raised by the theology of religions and which is still awaiting a final answer must find an answer, so that a position can be developed over against the other religions. Here the present situation of the religions itself already influences the way towards this answer.

5. European Christianity will markedly change in character as a result of the presence of other religions in Europe.

It is to be expected that the religious majorities in Europe will change in the medium to long term. But quite apart from the statistics, the encounter with other religions will increasingly mean that the Christian churches will change to a significant degree. Traditional elements must give way to new forms.

6. This will give Christianity a unique opportunity to bear witness to its principles in the encounter with other religions.

In their contact with the other religions in Europe, perhaps for the first time the Christian churches have an opportunity to live out their doctrine on a broad level in the face of other religions and thus avoid the mistakes which have often been made in the history of attempts at mission. In this way the churches can give an authentic testimony to what is central for them.

7. A possible failure of other religions to observe these principles is no reason for deviating from them.

The principles of Christian existence in a modern society – like freedom, equal rights, respect for human rights – are also indispensable in encounters with others. No relativizing of these principles is permissible even towards those who do not recognize them. They must be proved to be valid at the very point where they are disputed.

Translated by John Bowden

Notes

1. Cf. Michael Biehl, 'Religionen in Hamburg', *Ost-West. Europäische Perspektiven* 4, 2003, pp. 67–73: 72.
2. Cf. e. g. *Nostra Aetate 1; 2*.
3. The World Missionary Conference in Mexico City in 1963 described the change from a Western mission to a world mission with the formula 'mission in six continents', R. Frieling, *Der Weg des ökumenischen Gedankens,* Göttingen 1992, p. 269.

IV. Excursuses

Post-Communist Europe and the Continued Existence of Atheism

MIKLÓS TOMKA

I. Religion as resistance

The amputated parts have been stitched back on. Europe is gradually regaining its old dimensions. It can breathe with both lungs. A historical error has been corrected. But the wounds are not yet healed. It will take several generations before Communist totalitarianism with millions of dead, with the destruction of the fabric of society and the culture that had been taken for granted, simply becomes history. Europeans, indeed people the world over, need new experiences of togetherness before the people of Eastern Europe can forget that they were delivered over, against their will, by the great powers, including the European powers, to the unbridled power of the Soviet Union. Memories of the impotence they experienced, of being made objects of a cruel political experiment, burden half a continent. Both humanity and the social system were equally violated. Religion and the churches were of course also drawn into the suffering. At the same time they remained the most powerful force in the implicit, cultural and social, sometimes also institutional, organized resistance to totalitarianism, the only public social institutions which were not completely and utterly taken over.

II. Atheism and religion: social markers

The 'Communist Europe' of the second half of the twentieth century was an artificial construction made up of many different parts. Pre-modern and highly modernized societies lived side by side, with every different shade between them. Another invisible cultural dividing line also ran through the Communist camp. Some countries of the Soviet block had churches in the Eastern tradition, others had churches in the Western tradition. The former had little historical experience of the social and cultural differentiation that countries further west had experienced in the Investiture Dispute, the Renaissance, the Reformation and the Enlightenment. Accordingly traditions and mental predispositions differed. Not least, the social rooting of the churches was different. In Poland the church organization could keep its independence over against the party state. In other countries the power of the religious organization was broken or forced to bend the knee. In Poland religious expression remained almost synonymous with being a member of the church; in other countries religious expression often developed without any integration and control being provided by the institution. (The special case of Poland is analysed at greater length elsewhere; here I shall be reflecting primarily on other states and societies.)

Despite shared experiences of suffering the majority of people were not all on the same level. Deep splits can also be detected within individual societies. Brute force and a strategy of social selection produced high proportions of non-believers and atheists, often with power and influence, in all the former Communist states. Even after 1989 their existence is a fact. Over against this stands a turn towards religion which can be seen everywhere and which is dominant in many countries. Atheism and religion have become social markers, factors in polarization.

III. The sects

Especially in the West, people are fond of talking of the 'religious revival'. In reality, while the facts attest a substantial increase of interest in religion, a larger increase in participation in the life of the church is less widespread. Many observers claim to detect an explosion of sects as an alternative tendency. In fact the numbers of churches or sects being registered in many countries are increasing at breakneck speed, as are the numbers of registered communities, though not of their members. It is hard to deny that institutions are breaking up. However, this should not be thought to mean that the sects are gaining ground, as they are in Latin America. If we also take into account the revival of old nationalistic religions and a certain fascination exercised by New Age and Buddhism, it is possible only to say that the traditional churches are not proving able to attract and integrate the religious interest that is emerging.

IV. The different meanings of the choice of religion

However, what is presumably the most significant dispute rages over the conception of religion and religious expression. For many people it is a fundamentally personal decision, a right of the individual, which safeguards public life but is as far as possible to be kept out of it. This view is a minority position in what was formerly Communist Europe, but it is quite a powerful one. For the majority, religion is above all the vehicle of collective memories and the backbone of national identity, which has a great responsibility for the healing and humanization of society and for enabling the development of autonomous individuality. This expectation is given added weight by the fact that the church is numerically the strongest grouping within a diverse society which has been deprived of its former organic social ties. It is also one of the most important institutional networks, with high social prestige and also high demands for reparations. In public the two notions of religion and church are evidently based on different views of human beings and societies and have very different consequences in social action. From this point on the question of religion has become a topical, burning political issue, a sphere of opposed interests.

Occasionally this problem is dismissed as an anachronism. Ethnic, historical and collective identities, especially the nation, are said to be obsolete historical entities. However, such a criticism overlooks the social reality of Eastern Europe. Individuals need ties and groups if their identity is to mature. But in Eastern Europe a divided society is at least in the making. Processes of modernization and the party state have destroyed its pre-war structures. In addition, it has a problem with the integration of state and society. The vast majority of states in the region attained independence only after the First World War, or even only after the collapse of the Soviet empire. National myths of a former greatness and of alleged historical continuities are meant to serve to legitimate this inwardly and provide the foundation for a civic ethos. One may mock myths, but they are motivated by harsh realities. There is a wide gap between the desires of Eastern Europeans for a better life and the opportunities for achieving it. It does not take much of a stretch of the imagination to generalize from the disadvantaged, perhaps hopeless, situation of the individual to the fate of the whole people. In Eastern Europe people feel that they are a collective persecuted by history and discriminated against by more powerful nations. They share a sense of feeling excluded from the history of European development and this, together with a lower GDP compared with the richer Western countries, is a powerful factor in an inward-looking nationalism. It is poisonous, yet at the same time it is a basis for identity. The nation, the tradition, the specific culture and indeed religion are elements which define social belonging and also offer a basis for personhood. The question is whether there are other ways of getting out by one's own efforts of a situation which both individually and communally is historically, geopolitically and economically disadvantageous, or at least of coping with it psychologically. In Eastern Europe today at any rate the nation and religion make an important contribution towards shaping a social and individual identity which is confronted with this problem.

V. The power of the social context in the choice of religion

As a result of the tensions and developments mentioned above, four currents of different strengths come together in an ideological field of force which is seldom differentiated. In Eastern Europe there are still large areas where life is lived in a traditional way. Here the vigour of popular religion differs from country to country, but overall its importance is not to be underestimated. It can set plausibilities and certainties of tradition over against the contingencies of life. It is inextricably bound up with local communities and everyday culture. At a time when totalitarianism sought to grind down and prevent any social independence, the religious tradition cultivated by communities often remained the only framework in which people could understand themselves in a historical and social context (one which was not exclusively limited to the material). Over and above confessional differences, the religion of the people also continues to be the numerically dominant form of religion in Eastern Europe; simply because of its wide dissemination it also continues to be significant in a Europe in process of unification.

Beyond question there is little reflection on this kind of religion of individuals. It is more a matter of milieu and a system of social regulation than of personal decision. It is not completely under the control of the institutional church, but steeped in naive and superstitious interpretations. It is part of an agrarian culture, the 'religion of the village', and of a pre-modern experience of the world. It is not in accord with modern scientific thought. It offers many points of attack for the critique of the Enlightenment and indeed of theologians. Sociologists would describe it as a cultural time warp. However, instead of pointing a finger at these co-ordinates, we should accept them. This kind of religion is in harmony with the historical, economic and social situation of Eastern Europe. In particular it belongs to the primary reality of Orthodoxy. But its simple thought structure is also reproduced in the Communist ideology of past decades. The simplification and assertion of certainties to which there is no alternative also lives on in the view of some sects.

VI. Old and new religions

There are good arguments to suggest that this way of thinking will in time become obsolete. However, here time does not mean the clock or the calendar, but forms of social development. We may hope that collective disadvantages and social encapsulation will disappear. But experience teaches that new forms will also arise. At all events the waning of a pre-modern religion must be connected with economic and civic development and with the process of individualization in Eastern Europe. The pace of this development will not be determined simply by people in this region themselves.

At the centre of another significant type of Eastern European religion we find not tradition, but a knowledge which has been gained independently and under the harshest conditions. This type feeds on the experience of persecution. It has been existentially authenticated and reinforced in suffering and resistance. The witness of many people made it a superior force before the turning point of the abolition of Communism and today it is contributing to the blossoming of religious feeling. However, it has two weak points. It grew out of the religion of the pre-Communist era and was fixated on defending that religion. After the collapse of Communism some of the surviving witnesses of the church are no longer capable of accepting the demands of a contemporary Christianity. An exclusively and irrevocably pre-conciliar religious sensibility defended and tested with much sacrifice can hardly now struggle through to an *aggiornamento*. This kind of religion runs the risk of becoming fossilized in tradition, losing itself in nostalgia and sweepingly condemning the world and modernity – in particular believers and non-believers in the West.

The other weak point exacerbates the problem. Communism could not prevent the comprehensive functioning of the organization of the church. Here smaller communities and groups gained significance. They activated individuals to find a basis for their faith and to cultivate it independently. Especially in urban circles, among younger people and academics, religion became a goal and an instrument for offering inward resistance to totalitarianism. Friends and acquaintances strengthened one another in their conviction, though often none of them had any religious knowledge based on fact. The formation of such communities quite often led on the one hand to the sense of being an élite and on the other to strange heterodox positions of faith.

VII. The other side of the coin

Religious sensibilities old and new are only one side of the coin. Communism is not instinctively associated either with popular religion or with religion as a means of resistance, but with atheism. However, we need to be very careful in using this word. In Eastern Europe atheism was and always remained an exception, a standpoint adopted by propagandists and salaried demagogues. An indifference to religion and a trust in science are characteristic of large stretches of the population, especially the working class and the former leadership élite.

Communism excluded religion from public life, from education and public culture. The party state was able to restrict normal pastoral activities by closing churches, banning religious orders and institutions, harassing priests and so on. Mobility, urbanization and industrialization weakened the tradition and power of inherited social ties. Finally, by a combination of reprisals and rewards, upwardly mobile individuals and groups could be kept from practising religion in any way. Children were not baptized. Even if grandmothers brought them to the font, often they never saw the inside of a church again. Textbooks and the media disseminated malicious nonsense about religion and the churches.

Even the faithful forfeited much of their religious culture. An ever-increasing number of non-believers grew up with no knowledge of explicit, historically formed, institutional religion and with no ties to it. Religion has no meaning in their lives. Because they have no need for religion, they are not edified by its social presence either. Generally speaking, however, they are neither for nor against religion. Tensions arise only when they feel that the claims of the churches or believers are excessive. Thus it can be a cause for dispute if moral norms for the whole of society are formulated on a Christian basis or if the churches see themselves – in accordance with the self-understanding of Christians and many people whose thought is conservative – as guardians of the tradition or of basic values. It is like a red rag to a bull for otherwise peaceful non-believers if conservative politicians state as their aim the creation of a 'Christian Slovakia', a 'Christian Hungary' or a 'Christian Bulgaria', and so on . Behind this they suspect the rejection of pluralism and the human rights of non-believers generally. A dispute can also arise over the church's claim for reparations. One of the successes of the Communist information policy was that in all the countries of the region large parts of the population did not notice the persecution of religion and the church and now doubt that it ever happened. And if the churches are thought not to have suffered any particular disadvantages, their claims for reparations are also unfounded.

For decades non-believers were cut off from religious information and from information about believers. Any ideas they had were usually false. The big change and the gradual growth of the social presence of religion, the churches and believers – and the impact that this made on society – came as a shock to non-believers. This shock is still not under control. Conversely, in Communism many people with a folk religion which had not been thought out, including the majority of the clergy, thought that secularization would be overcome along with the spectre of totalitarianism. The unchanged high proportion of non-believers and especially their power is still hard for Christians to swallow. Now each party feels constrained by the other. Both think that the other came to achieve its social and political weight illegitimately. Both understand the present situation to be provisional. Both want to return to what in their view is the 'right order'.

VIII. Limits and prospects for religion in Eastern Europe

All in all, there is a deep polarization in Eastern Europe on the question of religion, sometimes even a militant mood. The balance of power differs greatly from country to country. In Romania religious feeling resembles that in Poland and there is almost a state church. In Slovenia a political secularism rules. In the Eastern states of Germany and in the Czech Republic non-believers are in the majority, while in Slovakia, Hungary and Croatia the situation is reversed. Even within individual countries there are occasionally very sharp differences. West Ukraine has kept an unbroken folk religion with believers amounting to almost 100% of the population, but more than half the population of East Ukraine is unchurched. The collapse of Communism and the hour of truth, which also came for religion, has led everywhere to new demarcations, to political and economic rivalries and confrontations.

The situation also compels Christians and the churches to define their socio-political and pastoral positions. The political factors which bring division seem to be of great importance everywhere. The claims for reparations, institutions and a say in public affairs often weigh more heavily than a sense of service and mission for all, both believers and non-believers. In several countries there are groups of academics who want to act as mediators, but who get into hot water because they cannot place themselves adequately in the situation of the organized church or the large group with a traditional mentality. So the tug-of-war goes on. It has not even become clear that several tasks have to be coped with at the same time if a solution is to be achieved.

Both believers and non-believers must agree to recognize the existence of the other group and acknowledge its rights to its own position. That includes a clear renunciation of an ideological state. For Christians that should not just be a political opportunity but a fundamental position of Christian faith.

Different values, interests and efforts are normal elements of a plural society. They must not be understood to be either illegitimate or to be declarations of war. Rivalry and competition must be accepted, and people must learn to settle their differences peacefully. Christians and the churches must struggle to establish their ideas in competition with politics, the media and other forces.

Eastern Europe is an area of headlong social change. The last traditional social structures are now breaking up and new ones are coming into being. Traditional regulations are being done away with through individualization. This is putting in question the long-dominant form of religion. That does not contradict the fact that the popular piety which lives on in many places contains treasures which can be cultivated and brought into the modern world – provided that social development is affirmed and supported. Thus the traditional parts of the churches have a great opportunity, but they will have to change their spots if they are going to perceive it.

Under Communism the churches were able to maintain well-constructed sub-cultures. When Communism ended these continued to prosper and were given further institutional support. Now the churches are realizing that as a result they have isolated themselves from other elements of society, not least from the urban middle classes and young people. But the fulfilment of the Christian mission calls for a dialogue with all parts of society and a presence in them. It is not enough to accept the existence of other trends, parties, sub-cultures and ideologies. Proclamation calls for a living relationship of trust with all groups, an appropriation of other ways of thinking and patterns of speech. This relationship must be established without attaching too much importance to old wounds which have not yet healed and new ones which are being inflicted.

A church which is not up to these tasks runs the risk (in some countries) of becoming the tool of the state church and/or a civil religion which is now coming into being, or (in other countries) of being satisfied with itself and in a sectarian way making itself remote from the majority of society.

Thus post-Communist Europe is displaying almost diametrically opposed phenomena. It is introducing to a European community on the one hand premodern social conditions and large numbers of people whose piety is an unreconstructed folk religion. On the other hand, at the same time large groups of people are appearing from Eastern Europe who have not been part of any religious and cultural condition and thus find it much easier to link up with European secularism than with the European tradition. The picture is further complicated by the fact that against the background of this contrast the move towards religion in Eastern Europe is seen in a very positive light. Peter Berger, the theorist of secularization, called Western Europe the dead end of Christianity because of its high degree of de-Christianization. Other winds are blowing in Eastern Europe.

Translated by John Bowden

Russia: Europe or not?

VLADIMIR FEDOROV

'We cannot reject Europe. Europe is our second motherland. I am the first to say so with all passion and have always been saying so. To us all, Europe is nearly as dear as Russia . . .'

Dostoyevsky

'So, is Russia a part of Europe? . . . Whatever. Maybe, it is and, then again, maybe, it isn't. I should say, sooner than not, it is a part of Europe to a degree. As much a part of it as anyone wants to recognize. However, the way we look at it now, there is indeed no Europe and what we call so is just a peninsula at the western end of Asia . . . Is really this glamorous word, Europe, an empty word void of exact meaning? Oh, ho! Of course not! Its meaning is very definite. It is, however, not of geography but of culture and history . . .'

Danilevsky

The question of the relationship between Russia and Europe, whether Russia is a part of Europe, has been discussed for centuries. Yet even now there is and may be no definite answer to it without first defining the inner concepts and context of this discussion. For instance, the present context of it is clear, if what we are discussing is European integration after the existing model of the European Union. If such is the case, then the formal criteria of admission to the Union are clear. However, even this kind of discussion can hardly ignore the cultural, historical, and spiritual or religious contexts. This is why many Europeans, and not just Russovites, are bewildered by the likelihood of Turkey's joining the EU, while for Russia it remains a remote possibility. To understand why they are bewildered, one must, after all, listen to the answers already given and discussed both in Russia and Europe.

We could say that the new criterion or factor in the discussion, besides economical and legal factors, is the degree of our being ecumenical, the readiness of every religion to strive for unity, including Christian unity, and preparedness for a peaceful inter-religious dialogue and co-operation, which means the ability of being consciously tolerant and seeing religious pluralism as a value. And this is exactly what is new, which, undoubtedly, is the achievement of twentieth-century Europe and which is still alien to Russia. In this sense, Russia is not yet a part of Europe. In this same sense, we could say that neither is Russia a part of Asia, where there is a tradition of religious pluralism. One may object, referring to the centuries-long experience of the Russian Empire where Christians and Muslims co-existed quite happily. Examples may be called to mind of some remarkable high-level meetings between representatives of various religions which have taken place in Russia lately. But regretfully, the ecumenical situation in Russia is at present still immature and socially disadvantageous. Let us not, however, stray away from the question: is or isn't Russia a part of Europe?

I. Danilevsky's answers

Probably, the most well known in Russia and the most thorough answer to this question was given, in his book, by N. Danilevsky, a philosopher and a scholar specializing in natural history and cultural studies. While the second edition of 1200 copies which left the print shop in 1871 was never completely sold out before the author's death in 1885, the 90,000 copies which came out in 1990 were sold in no time at all. This, of course, illustrates the urgency of the matter today and the continuing significance of the author's position. The book was subtitled 'A View of the Cultural and Political Relationships between the Slavic and Romano-German Worlds'. For the first time in the world, a scholar analysed civilizations, including that of Russia, as if anticipating the later works by G. Schmoller, A. Toinby, and L. Gumilyov.

The work was very highly regarded by Pitirim Sorokin, a famous Russian sociologist and cultural researcher who, after 1923, lived in the USA. He wrote: '[The book] that begins as a political pamphlet of the highest level shows a political discussion of such quality that it may be viewed as an outstanding treatise in philosophy, history, and the sociology of culture, and it ends in an example of an extremely penetrating and, in essence, true political prognosis and homily'. Of course, today, 130 years later, we cannot agree with every word in the book. For instance, the China and India which Danilevsky also wrote about are no longer dying civilizations and are undergoing a lot of renovation. Japan, which used to be not worth mentioning, is now emerging as a centre of a civilization of its own kind.

I think that the idea of creating a Slavic Union described in the closing chapters of the book is hardly productive today to any degree at all, yet it is exactly what now attracts certain nationalist circles. However, Danilevsky's ideas about the equilibrium between the West and the East are rather interesting and contemporary. He wrote: '. . . therefore, progress is not an exclusive prerogative of the West or Europe, while stagnation is not exclusively found in the East or Asia. Both are just among the characteristics of the age of a nation, wherever it lives, wherever its civic consciousness develops, and whatever its ethnic roots. Therefore, if indeed Asia and Europe, the East and the West were singular sharply defined units, even then belonging to the East or Asia could not be considered a stigma of being an outcast.'

Danilevsky, considering Europe as the Romano-German civilization, affirms that Russia 'was not nourished by any of the roots that delivered both beneficial and harmful juices to Europe, directly from the soil of the ancient world it destroyed. Neither was she (Russia) fed by the roots that supplied nourishment from the depths of the German spirit. She was no part of the reanimated Roman Empire of Charles the Great, which appears to have been as if a common stock whose offshoots made up the many branches of the European tree . . . Russia neither knew the yoke of nor was educated by scholasticism. Neither did she know the freedom of thought that brought about the new science nor lived by the ideals that became embodied in Romano-German art. To put it briefly, she neither partook of the European evil nor of the European good. So how on earth can she be a part of Europe? Neither her true modesty nor her true pride allow Russia to count herself among the European nations. She does not deserve this honour and, wishing to deserve another one, must never claim what is not hers.'

Neither did Danilevsky find it possible to recognize the relationship between Russia and Europe as the adoption of the former by the latter. He wrote: 'Somehow, we do not see any parental feelings in Europe's treatment of Russia. The point is not the feelings, however, but the very possibility of such an adoption.' Speaking of an engraftment seems more in order: 'Europe has been engrafted on to the wild tree of Russia . . . In this case, the appropriate motto is "Europaeus sum et nihil, europaei a me alienum esse puto". All European interests must become those of Russia. We must be consistent and recognize European wishes and aspirations as our own for, being a part of Europe, a country may have her separate disagreements with Germany, France, England or Italy. Yet there is no way she can disagree with Europe, that is, herself. She must reject everything that the whole of Europe finds alien and incompatible with its aspirations and interests and remain consistently true to the status she adopts.'

The ambiguity of Danilevsky's answer is not surprising. For ages, there has been a certain tension between Russia and the rest of Europe, which is the duality of the treatment of Europe by Russians, especially Russian intellectuals. There is a kind of symbiosis here, in which attraction and rejection, admiration and dislike, the use of European experiences and a claim for uniqueness are brought together. This duality conspicuously surfaces during crucial periods in Russia's history. And this duality is, in many respects, the result of the very duality of Europe's treatment of Russia. As Danilevsky put it, 'Whatever the difference of interests that tears Europe apart, these interests all have animosity toward Russia in common.' And moreover: 'The point is, Europe does not count us among her own . . . Europe sees Russia and all Slavs not just as alien but also as hostile . . . To them, no Russian may claim human dignity before he or she has completely lost his or her national identity . . .'. Today, we may call it the system of double standards.

II. Russia and Europe: ties and resistances

Yet one cannot say that there was a negative consensus in Western Europe, at the time Danilevsky published his book, concerning the idea of the Europeanization of Russia. In his book published in Germany in 1988, Professor Brueckner of the Derpt University gave a comprehensive and objective review of a large number of cultural and historical phenomena, beginning from old Moscow Russia, from long before Peter the Great, to our time, in which he considered the innovations introduced by Peter as just a more powerful push towards the goal that had been set long before him. This is how, in his introduction, the author summarized the viewpoint he expressed in the book: 'The joining by the Russians of the European family of nations was among the most important phenomena in the history of Western Europe. It was no less important as a part of the history of the world . . . the Slavs joined the Germans and Romans as an equal political factor; The Greek Orthodox world joined the Catholic and Protestant worlds. While expanding far to the West with the discovery of the New World, the area of historical development also largely expanded to the East . . . Russia's joining of the West was vitally important for her development. Everything depended on whether or not the Tzardom would enter into a relationship with Europe.

Because of the expansivity of European civilization as a natural force, because Russians proved so receptive towards the fruits of progress, the fact that the West had tried, sometimes, to keep the Russians away from participating in common development and forced them to stay at a lower stage of culture was of no importance. The fact that even now, in Russia, one can see relapses into the rejection of Europe is of no importance either. No government, leader or party may be credited with or, if one puts it this way, accused of the Europeanization of Russia. No individual or group of individuals can undo the process that has been underway for a long time.'

As in the nineteenth century, so early in the twenty-first century, the ambiguity of answers to the questions which have been raised persists in both Russia and Europe. However, at this time, the conviction that 'Russia has always been and will remain a European country . . . she belongs to the Christian world of Europe, while her 1000–year-long history is an integral part of the European process' is sufficiently widespread among Russia's political scientists, scholars, politicians, and intelligentsia. And further: 'While there is a great ethnic mixture in Russia, what is fundamental is the European cultural code. European ideals as well as European science and art possess the hearts and minds of the Russovites. In some way or other, the history of Europe has been imprinted on Russian self-consciousness and has affected the forming of Russia as a state and a nation. We are tied together by our common spiritual striving and the common ideals of the good and beauty. The destiny of Europe is also our destiny.'

III. Between Europe and Asia

There is a book entitled 'Europe: The Past, Present, Future' which deals with the principal tendencies in the economic, political, social, and cultural development of Europe late in the twentieth and early in the twenty-first centuries, the place and role of Europe in the present multi-polar world and its contribution to the globalization of economy, the forming of the new political system and world security. The Russian scholars who wrote it are very definite in asserting that 'Russia has always been and will remain a part of Europe' and that 'Russia is organic to and inseparable from the European civilization.' However, they are also certain that 'Russia, besides being a part of Europe, is also a part of Asia.'

These assertions as well as the experience of the economic and political development of Russia over the past fifteen years show that what N. Danilevsky wrote remains just as topical and just as ambiguous. Russia's public, that is, its academic élite begin, slowly but surely, to understand that the results of the next attempt at the fast Westernization of the country have proved just as painful and conflicting, at the very least, as the results of all the previous similar attempts because, as the very liberal-democratic reformers of economy who made it admit, no 'democracy could be won fast. So, what's the outcome? The outcome is the chaotic redistribution of property and power and their concentration at the one end, and the growth of poverty at the other.' Many have come to believe that Russia is beyond redemption and that prosperity is just not her lot because such is the Russian national character and culture, which, as these many believe, cannot be changed.

IV. So far away, so close

In 2003, in Russia, in connection with St Petersburg's tercentenary celebrations, discussions about the place of Russia in Europe and the importance of Europe to Russia once again became louder and more frequent. What is important to note, however, is the fact that Russia was not attracted to Europe because of the reforms of Peter the Great. Actually the attraction is as old as Russian statehood. 'The state created in mid-ninth century at the eastern end of Europe by Ryurick's descendants was no less a part of Europe than Poland Czechia, Pannonia (Hungary), or Serbia, all appearing about the same time.' Ancient Russia, mostly alien to the traditions of classical enlightenment, had close relations with the Western European world. Russian princes were often related to Western kings. Besides Byzantine art, Russia knew that of Western Europe. Mongolian onslaught interrupted these relations with the West. Yet they were renewed when, in the fifteenth century, a new political force appeared in Moscow, adopting the heritage of fallen Byzantium. Westerners would often find employment in Russia. However, Western travellers visiting 'Moskovia' usually saw it as a barbaric country and pointed to the crudity of local customs and the extreme ignorance of even the highest-placed Russians. Russia and Europe seemed to be two opposites. Religious intolerance was on the increase. To the eyes of a foreign Catholic, Russians were schismatic while Protestants found them primitively superstitious. Until the end of the seventeenth century, foreigners found interest in education extremely rare among the Russians. But even then, hundreds, then thousands of foreigners were recruited to work in various fields of Russian economy. Beginning in the reign of Peter the Great, who 'made a window into Europe' as Algarotti, a friend of Voltaire's put it, orientation towards Western Europe became an official policy. Love for Europe stopped being a sign of opposition and was no longer kept secret. It not only came into vogue but was now considered a necessary element of the outlook of an educated nobleman. All intellectuals of the time were, to some degree or other, promoters of all things European. The eighteenth century came as a 'peaceful' and relatively free time for the promoters of everything European. Gradually, European values were accepted by ever increasing numbers of Russians from all walks of life. The Russian state itself became the most important factor in the Europeanization of the country. From the time of Peter the Great, Russia rather actively meddled in European affairs, especially where the closest neighbours were concerned. Russia's ambassadors were now all over the place, while the Royal Court in St Petersburg developed marital relations with various German courts.

The reign of Catherine the Great gave the world a lot of new reasons to talk about Russia. The empress's personal qualities, her friendship with many outstanding thinkers of the time, and spectacular military victories, led to the appearance, in Europe, of whole collections of literary eulogies to Catherine. The intellectual part of the Russian nation made every effort 'to keep in step with the times where enlightenment was concerned'. The ideals of French enlighteners dramatically changed European spirituality and had numerous followers in Russia. These ideals were not just perceived intellectually but were considered as living manuals. Many noble families entrusted their children to French teachers, the followers of Voltaire. A whole mode of everyday and cultural behaviour formed that was considered appropriate for a freethinker (libertine). It naturally included active atheism, nihilistic attitudes towards all authorities, and freedom from publicly accepted moral norms. In the second half of the eighteenth century, in Russia, anticlerical sentiment was strong. The dramatic war against Napoleon, which touched upon the most significant interests of the European nations, made Alexander I 'the liberator of Europe'. His magnanimous treatment of France and even his role at the Vienna Congress made him very popular among Europeans. However, from the end of his reign, the European public again became hostile towards Russia. Over the second quarter of the century, European papers well mirrored this hostility. Reasons for that were numerous. Russia exerted a lot of pressure on the domestic policies of German states. Between the time of the Congresses and the events of the years 1848 and 1849, Russia put on a display that shocked Europeans. This included her hostility towards the July Monarchy in France, the suppression of the Polish uprising, etc. There was a lot of talk about 'pan-Slavic tendencies' and such. In Europe, Russia's political system was characterized as despotism, which was enough for many to believe in the existence of a threat from the East to European civilization itself and an impending new onslaught of Huns. Pan-Slavism could indeed pose such a threat. Everyone knew that there was no independent public opinion in Russia because the people were totally enslaved.

V. The challenge of the integration

Today, Europe's attitudes towards Russia are largely formed by factors of not just economic and cultural significance. In the nineteenth century, to a Russian thinker, the measures of true European civilization were 'literature that encompasses all the principal aspects of national life; science, which is free to explore and is widespread enough to serve the practical needs of the people; finally, such a degree of citizens' consciousness that makes public initiative a right and a custom'. While literature and science were not the factors that separated Russia from Europe, Pypin believes that '. . . here (as concerns the degree to which the citizens' consciousness is developed) the question concerning the Russian civilization and joining the cultured world becomes extremely complicated'.

Also, at this time, as already mentioned earlier in this article, the significant factor in Europe's potential for integration is ecumenical openness. I mean the general atmosphere, which is free from the false denominational stereotypes which result in tensions and conflicts. By these I mean first of all inter-confessional tensions within Christianity as a whole. However, the complete picture is larger and all inter-religious relations must be taken into consideration. This subject should be analysed in detail. So long as relations between the Orthodox and Catholic in Russia remain very cool, the success of integration remains doubtful. Anti-ecumenical attacks among the Orthodox are now less severe and the demands that the Russian Orthodox Church leave the World Council of Churches are heard less often. Yet the majority of both laypeople and clergy remain ecumenically ignorant. The document produced by the Russian Orthodox Synod in the year 2000 was oriented towards unity, yet there was no beneficial change in the situation. What is needed is a serious ecumenical strategy in theological and religious education. I would also like to mention the fact that there has been no interest displayed in Russia for the *Charta Oecumenica*. Despite having been among the creators of the document, the Russian Orthodox Church has never signed it.

As to the perspectives of ecumenical education, a parallel could be drawn with the passage from Dostoyevsky's writings which stands at the head of this article. 'Europe is our second motherland,' he wrote. According to Dostoyevsky, the first step on the way to unity must be '. . . for every one of us to become Russian, that is, one's own self. Once this happens everything will change. To become Russian means to stop despising one's own people. As soon as Europeans see that we have acquired respect for our own people and our own nationality, they will begin respecting us. Indeed, the more we develop our own national spirit, the closer we shall become to the souls of the Europeans. And once we become close to them, they will understand us much more easily.'

The fact that being ecumenical and open is not enough is the shortcoming of religious education as such. We still have not dropped ideology from our post-communist consciousness and haven't opened the values of our faith to those seeking them. We still do not fully carry out our Christian mission in post-totalitarian society. There are good signs, such as the 'Social Concept', yet there is still no openness and tolerance for other denominations and religions. There is no tolerance even for those in our own church whose opinions differ.

There is a lot of interest in Europe for Russian religious thought represented by, for example, such religious philosophers as Vladimir Solovyov. There is a lot of interest in those representing the Parisian theological school of the twentieth century. Indeed, the search for 'integral consciousness' or, as V. Solovyov put it, 'positive universal unity' has always prevailed in Russian philosophy. At the same time, however, the West has been reproached for the loss of spiritual integrity in life and the disintegration of cultural creativeness into separate, autonomous spheres, rooted in themselves. In the sharpest way, this thought was expressed by Ivan Kireyevsky in his article entitled 'The Enlightenment of Europe'. What proves that this criticism, with which many Russian philosophers agree, is not just fiction but is a cultural feature underlying Russian creativity and connected with the Russian spirit is the fact that Russia has almost never known art for art's sake. And many authors, such as Gogol, Tolstoy, and Dostoyevsky, hoped to bring it to perfection through Christian transfiguration. Regretfully, today, in Russia, many among the Orthodox are negatively disposed towards Solovyov and a number of other religious philosophers. This is the same phenomena of fundamentalism as the 'neophyte complex', and time and additional creative effort and resources are needed if we want to overcome this disease.

What is very important today for both Russia and Europe, for our common future, is the understanding of what helps integration and what impedes it. Religious values, which are not forced but manifest themselves in every act in life, form the foundation. At the same time, extremism in its every aggressive manifestation, be it called fundamentalism or anything else, is a stumbling block in the way of unity. In this connection, the call for the understanding of the necessity of *Ars Vivendi for the 20th century* proclaimed by Yuri Kagramanov is worth attention. He speaks about a search for uniting values. The examples he gives are Orthodoxy and Moslem Sufism. Yet, in the confessional sense, this *Ars vivendi* should be understood much more widely, as a value realized by a united Europe.

John Paul II, Poland and Europe

PATRICK MICHEL

In 1979, during his first visit to his native land, which at that time was part of 'the other Europe', John Paul II entrusted to 'the Polish pope, the Slavonic pope' the mission of manifesting 'the spiritual unity of Christian Europe which is indebted to the two great traditions of West and East: one faith, one baptism, one God and Father of all'. That said it all: Europe is one. And this Europe does not stop at Prague, Budapest or Krakow. For John Paul II, as Timothy Garton Ash noted in 1986, it extends 'beyond the Pripet marches to the historical limits of Eastern Europe, the Ukraine, Belarus and even the onion domes of Zagorsk'.[1] Above all, this one Europe is Christian. And it is one only because it is Christian.

Such a vision put in question the European equilibrium which derived from the balance of power at the end of the Second World War and thus constituted a formidable challenge to the Soviet system. Commenting in *Slavorum apostoli* on the work of Cyril and Methodius, proclaimed with St Benedict the patron saints of Europe (in a proclamation illustrating the conception of the 'two lungs' which allow the continent to breathe), John Paul saw here 'a decisive contribution to the building of Europe not only in the Christian religious communion but in the realms of its political and cultural union' and 'a prominent contribution to the formation of the common Christian roots of Europe ... which no serious attempt to reform the unity of the continent can ignore'.

I. The 'sign' of a Slavonic pope

When John Paul II became pope, this question of European unity seemed to be a purely abstract one. However, the particular status of his homeland inevitably attracted attention. An advance post of Latinity, Poland was also a society which tenaciously opposed Sovietization and in the process made Catholicism a symbol and banner of resistance. At the same time the church as an example of the incarnation of modernity, an authentic modernity, made it possible to challenge the criteria by which the regime claimed to legitimate itself, thought to be perverse by Poles. So over and above the novelty of the election of the first non-Italian pope for several centuries, beyond question the designation of Karol Wojtyla by the conclave represented an attempt by the universal church to make use of a specific case which could serve as an example and a model. The image it chose, however, was not so much that of Poland as a citadel under siege which could not offer itself the luxury of the culture of the doubt which was stifling the West and which the enterprise of the church had progressively dissolved, as that of a triumphant Catholicism (though this image drew its strength from the other image), operating at the centre of society and politics, regarded at the same time as being perfectly in phase with modernity, and forming a horizon by indicating, if not an 'after', at least a 'beyond'. When the church had seemed condemned to disappear by virtue of the emergence and development of the modern world, Poland, reversing the process, gave it back a place at the very heart of society, totally involved in it.

John Paul II's project of a 'new evangelization' thus pivots on the 'sign' given by the election of a Slavonic pope, and the collapse of Communism could seem to validate a reading which interpreted this designation of a Slavonic pope as a major moment in the reconquest of the world, starting at the very point where modernity had most manifestly demonstrated that it had gone mad. In the spirit of John Paul II, the victory of the church over atheistic Communism was supposed to anticipate that of religion over what had given birth to this Communism, namely 'this fight against God which to a large degree has dominated Western life and thought for three centuries'. After 1989, Christianity, having triumphed over the perverse, not to say barbarous, version of modernity necessarily had to take an interest in its 'civilized' version.

Rarely has a pontificate been organized so much by politics as that of John Paul II. It adopted one approach before 1989, focussed entirely on the idea that 'there cannot be a just Europe without the independence of Poland'; it adopted another afterwards, in which the opponent designated by John Paul 'democracy without values', democracy not informed by religion, gained prominence as the background against which Communism was disintegrating. The pope thus verified what was said by the Italian theologian Sergio Quinzio, namely that his problem was not that he was Polish, but that he was not Western.[2]

The device on which the 'new evangelization' turns is in fact based on an ambivalence which could only be made to work in and through politics. By making both the struggle and the victory over Communism the signs and stages of the broader process of a reconquest of a modern world which had escaped the grip of the church (and which consequently was inward-looking and going to its doom), John Paul II played on this imbalance, presenting the Soviet system as a barbarian version of political modernity, when in fact it was its very negation. The scheme to be found in the East was not that of a struggle between religion on the one hand and totalitarianism on the other. It was rather the use by society of the reference to an absolute to bring out (and question) the claim to have the power to pride itself on a 'totality'.

II. Human rights 'the prime duty of the church'

This ambivalence is essentially related to human rights. In 1975 Cardinal Wojtyla made their defence 'the prime duty' of the church, apparently in opposition to a secular tradition which presented human rights as an instrument of warfare against the rights of God. More specifically it relates to their content. When a platform of civil resistance was being built in Poland from the middle of the 1970s onwards, it was of course unnecessary for the different parties involved in it to spell out what they thought to be the 'human rights' which lay at its heart. It was enough to pretend that there was a consensus on this subject. In other words, the religious freedom of human beings could then serve as a symbolic recapitulation of human rights. There was evidently no urgent reason for disquiet on the part of the church over what the rights of non-believers could be in a Poland miraculously rid of Communism. But when this situation in fact materialized, the problem of the content of human rights inevitably had to take centre stage.

More generally, the use by the Poles of themes, symbols and discourse borrowed from the church did not necessarily entail the adoption of the categories which formed the basis for these themes, symbols and discourse. It was because power of a Soviet kind refused to integrate them ideologically that they became particularly effective. The church in Poland was little more than a function, the indication of a real relationship to pluralism (or if you like the indication of a relationship to 'real pluralism'): the church represented 'real pluralism' over against 'real socialism'. It played this role even more, and more clearly, than a reference to the nation – which to a certain point was susceptible to being exploited by the authorities. This was above all independent of the specific content of its categories, the sole importance of which was, to make the point once again, that they could not be integrated by those in power. In other words, their relevance, their performative character, was quite narrowly to function as an adversary who gave them meaning.

III. The risks of a 'democracy without values'

It was not in this neutral perspective that confusion appeared in John Paul II's position after the collapse of Communism. People already noted in *Centesimus annus* a certain degree of disillusionment over the situation in Central and Eastern Europe after 1989: these societies, which were supposed to anticipate the reconquest by the church of a sphere of Europe which the 'modern parenthesis' had forced it to abandon provisionally, in fact assumed all the shortcomings of their Western parallels. Thus in the large cities of Poland less than 30% of young people engage in religious practice and more than half are right outside any church influence. Certainly, 60% of young people say that they are believers, but that represents a drop of 30% from the end of the 1980s. Young people prefer to listen to their own consciences rather than obey Catholic norms. 70% of girls and 66% of boys accept contraception (as opposed to 35% and 46% respectively in 1988). More than 60% regard sexual relations before marriage as normal.[3]

It is in *Veritatis Splendor* that the disillusionment seems most evident, notably when John Paul II points out 'the risk of the alliance between democracy and ethical relativism', asserting that 'a democracy without values can easily be transformed into an explicit or disguised totalitarianism'. The pope counters this democracy without values with a triple reaffirmation, of universality, authority and the norm. Its form is familiar, participating simultaneously in a presence at the four corners of the world, the reiteration of Catholic truth, and the disqualification, in an often apocalyptic way, of 'societies and cultures strongly marked by the culture of death'. But just to criticize modernity is not sufficient to attest the existence of a space which it will no longer control, and any reaffirmation of the universal as a totality comes up against the evidence for the plural and the relative presented by the evolution of the world.

Once again, this includes Poland. As soon as the question of Europe began to be raised, the project of integration aroused lively emotions within the Catholic institution. The Polish bishops did not cease to emphasize the principle of respect for differences and the particular role that Poland would have to play in a united Europe. They certainly strove to speak with a single voice, referring to the pope, a decided supporter of Polish membership, but for all that did not succeed in disguising the differences between pro- and anti-Europeans within the episcopal conference. And the growing divisions within a pluralized Catholic population range from the denunciation by Radio Marya (with two million listeners) of 'the Europe of Sodom and

Gomorrah' to the appeal by John Paul II ('Poland needs the European Union and the European Union needs Poland').[4]

IV. Karol Wojtyla, the persistence of a model

In 1978 the election of a Pole to the papacy, marking a break, could not but constitute a sign and open up a mission. A quarter of a century later, beyond the heroic character of the involvement of the pope in the process which in his country and the rest of the block was to lead to the collapse of Communism, it is clear that over against the break which the sign announces can be set the evidence of continuity, of political ambivalence, of mission and finally of testing the limits. John Paul II in fact takes his place in the long line of those who have refused to 'become reconciled and negotiate' with modern civilization, a standpoint that his predecessor Pius IX had formulated in the middle of the nineteenth century. 'The death of a pope, the end of a tradition. The end of a tradition, the persistence of a model.' This was the diagnosis which Émile Poulat had already made just after Karol Wojtyla had succeeded to the papacy.

The European vision built on the sign represented by the election of a Slavonic pope in fact comes up against a two-fold reality, which the entry of Poland into the European Union (and the part played by John Paul II in the 2003 referendum) is far from hiding: the marked reticence of John Paul II towards the Orthodox, which was further confirmed on his visit to Greece in 2001, or his more recent visit to Croatia; and the resistance shown to him by European societies, notably evidenced by the debates over the drafting of the European Constitution (a constitution denounced by Jean-Louis Taran as 'an ideological operation which shows an authoritarian temptation to rewrite history'). All these elements signify the failure of the vision of a Europe whose unity would stem from its common Christian roots.

Translated by John Bowden

Notes

1. In 'L'Europe centrale existe-t-elle?', *Lettre Internationale*, Paris, autumn 1968, p. 5.
2. Sergio Quinzio, 'Le défi du pape Wojtyla', *Lettre Internationale*, Paris, winter 1990–91.
3. Tomasz Potkaj, 'Kosciol nie jest cool', *Tygodnik powszechny*, 22–29 December 2002, nos 51–52, p.13.
4. *Le Monde*, 10 June 2003.

DOCUMENTATION

Online Documentation on the Churches and Religions in the European Union

MASSIMO FAGGIOLI

I. Documents of COMECE (Commission of the Episcopal Conferences of the European Community)

COMECE, which came into being in 1980, is made up of the episcopal delegates of the national episcopal conferences of the countries of the European Union and has a permanent secretariat in Brussels. Austria, Belgium, England and Wales, France, Ireland, Italy, Germany, Greece, Luxembourg, the Netherlands, Portugal, Scandinavia, Scotland and Spain each have their own delegates, while the episcopal conferences of the Czech Republic, Hungary, Lithuania, Malta, Poland, Slovakia, Slovenia and Switzerland are associate members. The objective of COMECE, which meets in plenary session twice a year, is to monitor the political processes within the European Union Europea and to promote reflection on the challenges of European unity.

http://www.comece.org/upload/pdf/com_santiago_030509_fr.pdf: the declaration of 9 May 2003, *En route vers Saint-Jacques-de-Compostelle*, in view of the pilgrimage which COMECE is making to Santiago de Compostela in May 2004. The 2004 document is indicated as a fundamental moment in the history of united Europe and also for the role of the churches in Europe.

http://www.comece.org/upload/pdf/com_coeurs_030610_fr.pdf: the declaration entitled *Ouvrons nos coeurs. La responsabilité des Catholiques et le projet de l'Union Européenne*, which outlines the basic course of the construction of Europe in the period between 1989 and 2004, in particular between 2002 and 2004. The first part, on the principles of the Christian tradition, is followed by a second part on the declaration by Robert Schuman and a third part on the responsibility of Catholics in Europe.

II. Declarations by CEC (Conference of European Churches)

CEC is an association of 126 churches, Orthodox, Protestant, Anglican and Old Catholic, together with another 43 associated organizations on the European continent. The Roman Catholic Church is not a member of CEC, but has close relations with it. Founded in 1969, the CEC has a general assembly which meets at least every six years. The CEC has offices in Geneva, Brussels and Strasbourg. Together with CCEE, with which since 1971 it has had a joint committee which meets annually, it organized the first two European ecumenical assemblies (Basle 1989 and Graz 1997).

http://www.cec-kek.org/English/IntegrationprocE.htm: document of the working party on the process of European integration, *Churches in the Process of European Integration*, May 2001.

http://www.cec-kek.org/English/AdamisSpeech.pdf
http://www.cec-kek.org/English/vanBijsterfeld.pdf
http://www.cec-kek.org/English/Diamantopoulou.pdf
Speeches by M. Adamis (ambassador of the Slovakian mission to the EU), S. van Bijsterfeld (Catholic University of Tilburg) and A. Diamantopoulou (Commissioner Responsible for Employment and Social Affairs in the European Commission) at the seminar held in Brussels on 23–25 October 2003, on the EU Constitution and the Churches.

http://www.cecassembly.no: documents of the CEC assembly (25 June-2 July 2003 in Trondheim), including the Final Report, the first two chapters of which are devoted to 'Europe at a Crossroads' and 'Towards an EU Constitution'.

http://www.cec-kek.org/English/conpackwebindex.htm: documents with which CEC and especially its Working Group on European Integration has followed the work of the European Convention between March 2002 and March 2003; the Church of Greece, COMECE, Diakonisches Werk of the EKD-Diakonie, Eurodiaconia, the Evangelical Lutheran Church of Finland, the Evangelische Kirche in Deutschland (EKD) and the Quaker Council for European Affairs (QCEA) have made contributions to the discussion.

III. Activities of the CCEE (Council of the Episcopal Conferences of Europe)

Arising out of the collaboration between the episcopal conferences at Vatican II, the CCEE came into being in March 1971. It serves the episcopal conferences of Europe and seeks to promote collaboration between the bishops in Europe. All the presidents of the individual episcopal conferences of Europe are members of the CCEE, which now has 34 members. Together with the CEC, with which since 1971 it has had a joint committee, meeting annually, CCEE organized the first two European ecumenical assemblies (Basle 1989 and Graz 1997).

http://www.ccee.ch/english/press/berlino2.htm: *Building a Reconciled Europe*, conclusions of the meeting of the Secretary Generals of the thirty European episcopal conferences in Berlin from 24–28 May 2003), organized by CCEE to consider the question of the enlargement of the EU and the European Constitution.

http://www.ccee.ch/english/press/consultazioneo3fine.htm: *The Treasure of the Orient for the Churches and Europe*: information on the meeting held at Leányfalu (Budapest, 27–30 November 2003) with delegates from fifteen countries of central and eastern Europe, organized by CCEE and CEC.

http://www.ccee.ch/english/press/jk2004fine.htm: the document *CCEE and CEC Move Towards The Third European Ecumenical Assembly* dated 3 February 2004, on the activity of the CCEE together with the CEC in 2004 with a view to the third European ecumenical assembly planned for 2007.

http://www.ccee.ch/francais/domaines/comiteislam.htm: documents (1994–2003) of the CCEE/CEC committee on Islam en Europe relating to the role of the churches towards European Muslims in a pluralistic society and on the responsibilities and commitments of Christians and Muslims in Europe.

IV. Documents of the papal magisterium – John Paul II

http://www.vatican.va/holy_father/john_paul_ii/apost_exhortations/documents/hf_jp-ii_exh_20030628_ecclesia-in-europa_it.html: *Ecclesia in Europa*, post-synodal exhortation by John Paul II, dated 28 June 2003, a document which followed the second Synod of Bishops for Europe (10–23 October 1999).

V. Documents of the EKD - Evangelische Kirche in Deutschland

EKD brings together 23 Lutheran, Reformed and United churches of the German states, and also functions at a national level. Its organs are the synod, the council and the assembly.

http://www.ekd.de/bevollmaechtigter/bruessel/stellungnahmen_konvent_zukunft_europas.html: joint statement by the president of the German episcopal conference, Cardinal. K. Lehmann, and the president of the council of the EKD, M. Koch, dated 21 June 2002, on the future of Europe.

http://www.ekd.de/EKD-Texte/2096.html: documents containing the standpoints of the EKD on European questions (1997–2001).

VI. Documents of the Leuenberg Church Fellowship

The *Leuenberg Church Fellowship* came into being in 1973 with the Leuenberg Concord, which put an end to 450 years of division between the Lutheran and Reformed Churches. By 2004, 103 churches had signed the Concord; in addition to all the Reformation churches, the Waldensian Church and the European Methodist Churches are also members. It is made up of a general assembly (which meets every six years), an elected executive committee, a president and a secretariat.

http://lkg.jalb.de:8080/lkg/jsp/document.jsp?news_id=19&lang=en&side_id=36: standpoints of the executive committee of the Leuenberg Concord on the European Convention, 22 June 2002.

http://lkg.jalb.de:8080/lkg/jsp/document.jsp?news_id=24&lang=en&side_id=36: Standpoints of the Concord on the Convention on the Future of Europa, 22 June 2002.

http://lkg.jalb.de:8080/lkg/jsp/documentslist.jsp?lang=en&side_id=21&be=8: a list of the publications of the Leuenberg Concord on the churches in the future of Europe, including *Being Protestant in Europe* and *En route towards Europe* (2003).

VII. Documents of the churches which are signatories to the Porvoo agreement

The name Porvoo (Finland) denotes the final report of the conversations between official representativeof four Anglican churches and eight Nordic and Baltic churches between 1989 and 1992. The Porvoo Joint Declaration has been signed by the Churches of England, Ireland and Wales, the Episcopalian Church of Scotland, the Churches of Denmark, Norway and Sweden, and the Evangelical Lutheran Churches of Estonia, Finland, Iceland, Latvia and Lithuania. It is an instrument of the visible communion between the Anglican churches in the British Isles and other national churches in Europe.

http://www.porvoochurches.org/statements/en.htm: *The Porvoo Common Statement*, 1993, with a chapter 'Our Common Mission Today' centred on the role of the churches in the new Europe.

VIII. Statements and actions by Romani Prodi, President of the European Commission, and the group of policy advisers to the President

The group of policy advisers to President Prodi is a unit of the European commission which reports directly to the President. The 'Michalski group', which is co-ordinated by Professor K. Michalski of the *Institut für die Wissenschaften vom Menschen* (IWM) in Vienna and includes among others S. Ferrari, B. Geremek, M. Rocard and S. Veil, was formed by President Prodi to discuss European values.

http://europa.eu.int/comm/commissioners/prodi/pdf/spirit_statement_prodi_en.pdf: statement by Romano Prodi, President of the European Commission, on the report of the High Level Advisory Group, *Dialogue between Peoples and Cultures in the Euro-Mediterranean Area*.

http://europa.eu.int/comm/commissioners/prodi/pdf/michalski_210503_speech_prodi_en.pdf: speech by Romano Prodi, President of the European Commission, at the third meeting of the think-tank on the spiritual and cultural dimension of Europe, on 'The Role of Religion in European Integration' (Brussels, 21 May 2003).

http://europa.eu.int/comm/commissioners/prodi/pdf/spirit_report_en.

pdf: report by the High Level Advisory Group, dated October 2003, established on the initiative of Romano Prodi, President of the European Commission, *Dialogue between Peoples and Cultures in the Euro-Mediterranean Area*.

http://europa.eu.int/comm/dgs/policy_advisers/publications/seminar_anti_semitims/index_en.htm: *Europe, against Anti-Semitism for a Union of Diversity*: seminar organized under the auspices of the European Commission by the European Jewish Congress and the Congress of European Rabbis, Brussels, 19 February 2004.

http://europa.eu.int/comm/dgs/policy_advisers/activities/dialogue_religions_humanisms/events/index_en.htm: diary of meetings (2003) of the President's policy advisers with the churches and religions in Europe (including: European Council of Jewish Communities; European Council of Religion Leaders; European Conference of Grand-Imams; Pan-European Conference of the Greek Orthodox Church).

Translated by John Bowden

Contributors

JANET MARTIN SOSKICE is the University Reader in Philosophical Theology at the University of Cambridge. She is a past-president of the Catholic Theological Association of Great Britain and a member of the board of directors of *Concilium*.

Address: Faculty of Divinity, University of Cambridge, West Road, Cambridge CB3 9BS, England
E-mail: j.soskice@jesus.cam.ac.uk

ALBERTO MELLONI teaches contemporary history at the University of Modena and Reggio Emilia; he is a member of the John XXIII Foundation for Religious Studies in Bologna, on the board of *Cristianesimo nella storia*, and a member of the board of directors of *Concilium*. He has written extensively on the history and the institutions of Christianity from the Middle Ages (*Innocento IV*, preface by B.Tierney, Genoa 1990) to the twentieth century: he worked on John XXIII (*Tra Istanbul, Atene e la Guerra. A. G. Roncalli vicario e delegato apostolico 1935–1944*, Genoa 1993; *Il Giornale dell'anima di Giovanni XXIII*, Milan 2000); on Vatican II (as editor of the first five volumes of *Storia del concilio Vaticano II diretta da G.Alberigo*, Bologna 1995, 2001); on Vatican II diplomacy (*L'altra Roma, Politica e S.Sede durante Il concilio Vaticano II, 1959–1965*, Bologna 1999); and on the conclave (*Il conclave. Storia di una instituzione*, Bologna 2001). His articles in various journals are devoted to the interplay between politics and religion.

Address: Via Crespi 6, 421000 Reggio Emilia, Italy
E-mail: alberto.melloni@tin.it

ROMAN SIEBENROCK is professor at the Institute for Biblical Studies and Fundamental Theology in Innsbruck. He was born in 1957 and wrote his doctoral dissertation in Tübingen, on John Henry Newman. He is in charge of the Karl Rahner Archive and works on the question of God and introduction to theology. His publications include his Habilitationsschrift in fundamental theology, *Wer sich Gott naht, dem naht sich Gott. Studien zur Interpretation und Rezeption des Werkes Karl Rahners SJ in einer Zeit der 'anima technica vacua'*, Innsbruck 2000, and *Wahrheit, Gewissen und Geschichte. Eine systematisch-theologische Rekonstruktion des Wirkens John Henry Kardinal Newmans*, Internationale Cardinal Newman Studien XV, ed Heinrich Fries and Günter Biemer, Sigmaringendorf 1996.

Address: Karl-Rahner-Platz 1, A-6020 Innsbruck, Austria
E-mail: roman.siebenrock@uibk.ac.at

ERIK BORGMAN was born in Amsterdam in 1957; he is a lay Dominican, married, and the father of two daughters. He studied theology and philosophy from 1976 to 1984 at the Catholic University of Nijmegen, where he gained his doctorate in 1990 with a study on the significance of the different forms of liberation theology for university theology, *Sporen van de brevrijdende God*, Kampen 1990. Work with the Dutch Dominicans between 1989 and 2003 led to his biography *Edward Schillebeeckx: A Theologian in His History. Part I. A Catholic Theology of Culture (1914–1965)*, London and New York 2003. From 2001 he has been co-ordinator of the Theology and Humanities section of the interdisciplinary Heyendaal Institute of the Catholic Institute of Nijmegen, which focusses on theology, science and culture. He is also author of *Dominican Spirituality: An Exploration*, London and New York 2002. He is president of the International Society for Religion, Literature and Culture and editorial secretary of *Tijdschrift voor Theologie*, as well as being on the editorial board of *Concilium*.

Address: Heyendaal Institut, Erasmusplein 1, 6525 HT Nijmegen, The Netherlands
E-mail: E.Borgman@hey./kun.nl

SILVIO FERRARI is professor at the Faculty of Law in the University of Milan. He was born in 1948 and after gaining a degree in law at the Catholic University of Milan did postgraduate work at the British Library, the Hebrew University, Jerusalem, and Columbia University, New York. He taught church and state relations at the University of Parma from 1973–89 and ecclesiastical law at the University of Turin from 1990–94, and came to the State University of Milan in 1994. He has also taught church and state relations in the University of Louvain since 1998 and in the University of Strasbourg since 2000. His books include*: Ideologia e dogmatica nel diritto ecclesiastico italiano (1929–1979)*, Milan 1979; *Vaticano e Israele dal secondo* *conflitto mondiale alla guerra del Golfo*, Florence 1991; *Lo spirito dei diritti religiosi. Ebraismo, cristianesimo e islam a confronto*, Bologna 2002.

Address: Facoltà di Giurisprudenza, Università di Milano, Via Festa del Perdono 7, 20122 Milan, Italy
E-mail: silvio.ferrari@unimi.it

MICHAEL BRENNER is Professor of Jewish History and Culture at the University of Munich. His publications include: *Zionism: A Brief History*, Princeton 2003; *The Renaissance of Jewish Culture in Weimar Germany*, New Haven 1996; and, as co-author, *German-Jewish History in Modern Times*, New York 1997–98.

Address: Abteilung für Jüdische Geschichte und Kultur am Historischen Seminar der Ludwig-Maximilians-Universität München, Geschwister-Scholl-Platz 1, D-80539 Munich, Germany
E-mail: Michael.brenner@lrz.uni-muenchen.de

REINHARD FRIELING was Director of the Konfessionskundlichen Instituts des Evangelischen Bunds in Bensheim from 1981 to 1999. Since 1988 he has been honorary professor of systematic and ecumenical theology. He was a member of the synod of the Evangelical Church of Germany between 1984 and 2003 and president of its committee on Europe. He has been president of the study commission of the Conference of European Churches since 1993 and a member of the joint working party between the World Council of Churches and the Vatican from 1991 to 1999. He has written twenty books on ecumenism, most recently *Amt. Laie – Pfarrer – Priester – Bischof – Papst*, Ökumenische Studienhefte 13, Göttingen 2002; *Religionsunterricht und Konfessionen*, Bensheim 1999; and *Der Weg des ökumenischen Gedankens. Eine Ökumene-Kunde*, 1992.

Address: vor Hees Strasse 3, 64646 Heppenheim, Germany
E-mail: frieling.reinhart@t-online.de

KARL-JOSEF KUSCHEL was born in 1948. He studied German and theology at the universities of Bochum and Tübingen. He did his doctoral studies in Tübingen, where he was an academic assistant, and from 1981 to 1995 worked at the Institute for Ecumenical Research and the Catholic Faculty there. He is now Professor of Culture and Inter-Religious Dialogue in the University of Tübingen and Vice-President of the Global Ethic Foundation. Among his many works are: *Jesus in der deutsch-sprachige Gegenwartsliteratur* (1978); *Born Before All Time: The Dispute over Christ's Origin* (1992); *Laughter. A Theological Reflection* (1994); *Abraham: A Symbol of Hope for Jews, Christians and Muslims* (1995); *Vom Streit zum Wettstreit der Religionen. Lessing und die Herausforderung des Islam (*1998); *The Poet as Mirror* (1999); and *Jesus im Spiegel der Weltliteratur* (1999).

Address: Sandeckerstrasse 2, D 72070 Tübingen, Germany
E-mail : karljosef.kuschel@uni-tuebingen.de

JAMES K. VOISS SJ is a Jesuit priest of the Oregon Province, currently working as an Assistant Professor in the Department of Theological Studies at Saint Louis University. He completed his PhD at the University of Notre Dame in 2000 on *A Comparison and Analysis of Karl Rahner and Hans Urs von Balthasar on Structural Change in the Church.*

Address: 3601 Lindell Blvd, Saint Louis, MO 63108, USA
E-mail: voissj@slu.edu

THOMAS BREMER is Professor of Ecumenics and Peace Studies at the Catholic Theological Faculty of the University of Münster. He was born in 1957 and studied Catholic theology, Slavonic and classical philology in Munich and Belgrade; from 1985 to 1995 he worked at the (then) Catholic Ecumenical Institute of the University of Münster. In 1990 he gained his doctorate with a work on ecclesiology in the Serbian Orthodox Church. His research interests are Orthodoxy in Russia and Serbia, ecumenical relations between Western and Eastern churches, and churches and religious communities in situations of conflict. His publications include: *Ekklesiale Struktur und Ekklesiologie in der Serbischen Orthodoxen Kirche im 19. und 20. Jahrhundert*, Würzburg 1992; *Konfrontation statt Ökumene. Zur kirchlichen Situation in der Ukraine*, Erfurt 2001; *Kleine Geschichte der Religionen in Jugoslawien*, Freiburg 2003.

Address: Katholisch-Theologische Fakultät, Ökumenisches Institut Universität Münster, Hüfferstrasse 27, 48149 Münster, Germany
E-mail: th.bremer@uni-muenster.

MIKLÓS TOMKA was born in 1941; he studied in Budapest, Louvain and Leiden. He was a member of the editorial board of *Concilium* until 2004. He is professor of sociology of religion in Szeged, Hungary. He has also been visiting professor in Bamberg, Innsbruck and Salzburg. He is head of the Centre for Philosophy of Religion in the Institute of Philosophy of the Hungarian Academy of Sciences. A co-founder of the Hungarian Pastoral Institute (in 1989), he is also director of the Hungarian Religious Research Centre.

Address: H-1171 Budapest, Várviz u. 4, Hungary
E-mail: tomka@hcbc.hu

VLADIMIR FEDOROV is archpriest in St Petersburg. For ten years he has been Director of the Orthodox Institute of Missiology and Ecumenism and vice-rector of the Russian Christian Institute for Humanities. For the last two years he has been a consultant on Eastern and Central Europe for the WCC programme of ecumenical theological education. His publications include *Religion and Nationalism, St Petersburg, 'Apostolic City'*, 2000 (of which he is co-editor).

Address: PIMEN, 191002, Post Box 31, St Petersburg, Russia
E-mail: pimen@quantum.ru

PATRICK MICHEL gained a doctorate and a habilitation in political sciences and then from 1984 worked at the Centre d'Analyse comparative des Systèmes Politiques and at the Centre d'Étude Comparative de Politique Etrangère (Paris I Panthéon Sorbonne) from 1984 to 1989; he then worked at the Groupe de Sociologie des Religions (Iresco) from 1990 to 1993 and at the Centre d'Études Interdisciplinaires des Faits Religieux (EHESS) from 1994 to 2001. Director of research since 1996, he rejoined the Centre d'Études et de Recherches Internationales (CNRS-FNSP) in 2001. He is also in charge of courses at the Institut d'Études Politiques de Paris. Publications include *La société retrouvée – Politique et religion dans l'Europe soviétisée*, Paris 1988; *Politique et religion – La grande mutation*, Paris 1994; *La religion au musée*, Paris 1999.

Address: 68 rue La Fontaine, 75016 Paris, France
E-mail: patrick.michel@cnrs-dir.fr; pmichel@ceri-sciences-po.org

MASSIMO FAGGIOLI works at the Fondazione per le scienze religiose 'Giovanni XXIII', Bologna.

Address: Via San Vitale 114, 40125 Bologna, Italy
E-mail: massimofaggioli@libero.it

The editors thank the following for their help in preparing this issue:
N. Ancic, E. Barbieri Masini, C. Boureux, V. Elizondo, E. Farrugia, A. Ganoczy, C. Geffré, R. Gibellini, W. Jeanrond, E. Pace, D. Power, N. Reck, R. Siebert, L. Swidler, L. Vischer

CONCILIUM

FOUNDERS

A. van den Boogaard
P. Brand
Y. Congar OP †
H. Küng
J.-B. Metz
K. Rahner SJ †
E. Schillebeeckx OP

FOUNDATION

Jan Peters SJ
Ben van Baal
Eric Borgman
Alberto Melloni
Christoph Theobald SJ

DIRECTORS

Regina Ammicht-Quinn (Frankfurt, Germany)
Erik Borgman (Nijmegen, The Netherlands)
Christophe Boureux OP (Lyon, France)
Hille Haker (Cambridge MA, USA)
Maureen Junker-Kenny (Dublin, Ireland)
Solange Lefevbre (Montreal, Canada)
Alberto Melloni (Reggio Emilia, Italy)
Eloi Messi Mettogo (Yaoundé, Cameroun)
Janet Martin Soskice (Cambridge, UK)
Jon Sobrino SJ (San Salvador, El Salvador)
Luiz Carlos Susin (Porto Alegre, Brazil)
Elsa Tamez (San José, Costa Rica)
Christoph Theobald SJ (Paris, France)
Andrés Torres Queiruga (Santiago de Compostela, Spain)
Marie-Theres Wacker (Münster, Germany)
Elaine Wainwright (Auckland, New Zealand)
Felix Wilfred (Madras, India)
Ellen van Wolde (Tilburg, The Netherlands)

General Secretariat: Erasmusplein 1, 6525 HT Nijmegen, The Netherlands
http://www.concilium.org
Manager: Baroness Christine van Wijnbergen

Concilium Subscription Information

February   2004/1: *Original Sin*

April   2004/2: *Rethinking Europe*

June   2004/3: *The Structural Betrayal of Trust*

October   2004/4: *African Christianities*

December 2004/5: *Feminist Movements in Different Religions*

New subscribers: to receive *Concilium 2004* (five issues) anywhere in the world, please copy this form, complete it in block capitals and send it with your payment to the address below.

Please enter my subscription for *Concilium 2004*

Individuals
___ £32.50 UK/Rest of World
___ $63.00 North America

Institutions
___ £48.50 UK/Rest of World
___ $93.50 North America

Please add £17.50/$33.50 for airmail delivery

Payment Details:
Payment must accompany all orders and can be made by cheque or credit card
I enclose a cheque for £/$ _____ Payable to SCM-Canterbury Press Ltd
Please charge my Visa/MasterCard (Delete as appropriate) for £/$ _____
Credit card number _____
Expiry date _____
Signature of cardholder _____
Name on card _____
Telephone _____ E-mail _____

Send your order to *Concilium*, SCM-Canterbury Press Ltd
9–17 St Albans Place, London N1 ONX, UK
Tel +44 (0)20 7359 8033 Fax +44 (0)20 7359 0049
E-Mail: office@scm-canterburypress.co.uk

Customer service information:
All orders must be prepaid. Subscriptions are entered on an annual basis (i.e. January to December) No refunds on subscriptions will be made after the first issue of the Journal has been despatched. If you have any queries or require information about other payment methods, please contact our Customer services department.

BL
695
.R48
2004